Praise for THE
ACCIDENTAL ~~SOLOPRENEUR~~

"Most of the entrepreneurial stories we read are written about legendary entrepreneurs. While that's great, hindsight bias is strong. That means these stories rarely give a true account of the entrepreneurial journey.

Dennis Geelen's The Accidental Solopreneur is different. We get to follow along as Alex Green goes from burnt out corporate exec to a happy solopreneur. Alex's journey is messy—as is so common in real life—but it's also inspiring and hopeful.

Whether you're sick of climbing the corporate ladder and looking for a change or you're already in the depths of your entrepreneurship journey and seeking affirmation that you're on the right path, you'll find what you need in The Accidental Solopreneur."

Katelyn Bourgoin, CEO of Customer Camp

"Part entrepreneurial playbook and roadmap, part John Grisham page-turner. If you're in business to win, you won't be able to put it down.

This is a real-life book that feels as personal as an autobiography accompanied by practical real-life insights every entrepreneur needs to know to thrive in today's world. Brilliant. Congratulations."

David Brier, Award Winning Author of 'Brand Intervention'

"This is a must-read about finding your best life, about being open to a path less travelled that might liberate and empower you: solopreneurship. Our protagonist Alex's journey is one many of us can relate to where you question the value of climbing the proverbial corporate ladder, and the impact it has on work-life balance.

Is the tradeoff worth the toll to your mental and physical health? Family and friend time?

If chasing promotions for material things isn't what makes you truly happy or even content, we see through Alex that there is, indeed, another viable option to feeling burnout much of the time. We learn there comes incredible freedom from going out on your own, and challenging yourself to be resourceful, resilient, and adaptable in building your own venture.

He doesn't romanticize the transition from employee to entrepreneur yet the blueprint Alex shares with us shows us that by designing and shaping your own destiny, you—and everyone around you—will come out all the better for it."

Neil Morton, Serial Entrepreneur and Community Builder

"Weaved into an entertaining story, Dennis Geelen generously shares his insights and experience, helping everyone who considers going solo to get a head start. This book convinces through its brilliant combination of depth, relatability, and numerous practical and timeless lessons on building a sustainable and successful business from scratch. Whether you are playing with the idea of starting your own business or are an established business owner, pick up this book, learn, and save some sleepless nights."

Thomas Lahnthaler, Author of Navigating Beyond Crisis & Founder of The Crisis Compass and Groundwork

"Dennis Geelen does a fantastic job of bringing together the best bits of startup-solopreneur advice from both his own experiences and many trusted external sources, and cleverly crafts these into a believable and engaging parable containing characters that we can all relate to. When you combine these invaluable lessons weaved into the story, we're rewarded with a corporate-to-solopreneur transition playbook for success."

Karl Sandland, Founder of BrightCX LTD

"A timely and powerful story about the courage to change your career to improve your health, wellness, and happiness. Chronic stress and burnout are critical issues that impact more than an employee or workplace, but it impacts families who lose the mental and physical presence of a loved one. This is a must read for people needing the encouragement to create a different experience for themselves and their family."

Jennifer Dole, former software executive turned solopreneur

"Using storytelling from the point of view of a dissatisfied, ready-to-escape corporate leader, author Dennis Geelen draws the visual picture and thought pattern of the issues facing a new solopreneur. The wave of emotions and how it affects lifestyle choices is described, and lived, through the characters. Through the main character Alex's journey, we find the entrepreneurial spirit in us and root for his success. What a great read for anyone thinking of going out on their own!"

Sandra Lynn, Serial Entrepreneur / Consultant

"This beautiful story is about changing your life, taking pleasure in the beauty of 'enough,' and building a future as a solopreneur. In the journey from burnt-out executive to a successful and fulfilled solopreneur, Alex encounters many challenges to overcome and discovers that true happiness is not about achievements, but rather how you spend your time. This is a must read for anyone that wants to take control of their own destiny and become a solopreneur."

**Kevin McDonnell, CEO & Founder of
The Digital Health Consultancy**

"Dennis Geelen does an amazing job of crafting an engaging story that many people can relate to. They have struggled for years climbing the corporate ladder. They are burnt out. They want something different. If you are considering taking the leap into entrepreneurship, READ this book!"

**Daniel C. Burkholder, Entrepreneur /
Marketing Coach**

"This story of a burnt-out corporate employee is one that I instantly found myself relating to. Dennis does a great job highlighting the issues that many of us face in a corporate setting, how it spills over to family life, our health, and quality of life overall. He doesn't shy away from talking about the harsh realities of working for a company or working for yourself.

Having done it himself, Dennis is able to pull you into the main character's experiences, emotions, and internal struggles. Whether you're just starting out on your solopreneur journey or still in corporate considering the idea, this book will pave a path for you that you can start to walk on."

Pathik Parikh, Founder and CEO of Parikh Ventures LLC

"Not your average 'guide' on how to become a solopreneur. Dennis Geelen weaves vital lessons into a story that's as easy to read as it is practical. The book covers not only the shifts in marketing and perspectives as a business owner but also highlights the mindset shifts, which are often overlooked. Looking to create your own business, this book will provide you with the solid foundation to succeed."

Karen Grill, Persuasion Strategist & Business Coach

"Dennis Geelen takes you on the solopreneur's journey through the eyes of Alex, an overworked, overstressed corporate exec who steps out on his own to find peace and fulfillment. The story grabs you and pulls you in with relatable characters and emotional intensity. You experience first-hand the pivotal steps along the way. This is a roadmap for getting the life you want, told through a powerful, engaging narrative. Anyone looking for inspiration and guidance on the path to solopreneurship should read this book!"

Will Kersten, Copywriting and Messaging Strategist

The
Accidental Solopreneur

FROM BURN-OUT TO

FREEDOM

A PARABLE

DENNIS GEELEN

ISBN (soft cover) 978-1-7773266-6-1
ISBN (ebook) 978-1-7773266-7-8

Published by Zero In Publishing

Cover designed by MiblArt

Dennis Geelen is the founder of consulting company, Zero In, focusing on helping businesses be more customer centric and innovative.

Visit the Zero In website to find out more at www.zero-in.ca.

Geelen also works directly with solopreneurs to help them avoid all the mistakes he made when starting out.

To see how Dennis can help you on your journey, visit www.dennisgeelen.me

Contents

Introduction

Some people are meant to be employees. Aligned with the organization's vision and strategy and finding a nice niche for themselves within the business, these employees work hard and dedicate themselves to the company. They like the comfort and security of a regular paycheck. Over time, they may learn and grow and climb the corporate ladder. Or perhaps they enjoy their position and stay in it for their entire career. Businesses need these people. The world needs these people. I thrived for over twenty years as one of these people.

Some people are meant to be entrepreneurs. They don't like to be tied down by company rules and protocols. They want to create and build. They enjoy, maybe even relish, the risks that come with not having a regular paycheck. They crave the adrenaline rush that comes from creating an income-generating business from scratch. Businesses need new creative minds. The world needs these people. Surprisingly, I too became an entrepreneur eventually.

Some people seek the best of both worlds. So, they start a side hustle, which gives them the security of a corporate job while supplying an outlet to entertain their entrepreneurial side. One day, they may decide to turn their side hustle into a full-fledged business, leaving the corporate world behind. For some, it will forever remain a side hustle, either by choice—they prefer it that way—or by necessity—a lack of customers forces it to remain a side hustle.

Look at your current situation, and you can probably slot yourself into one of the categories above—employee, side hustler, or full-on entrepreneur. Maybe you're firmly entrenched in your corporate job and loving it. That's terrific! Or maybe you are at a point similar to where I once was, and you're seeing a change in yourself. Getting an itch to build something of your own. Although you've been working for years as a standard employee, you now have an entrepreneurial craving that needs quenching. Or maybe you have always been the entrepreneurial type. You may be at the very beginning of your journey, or you may be a few years into it already.

But there are two other types of people we should examine.

There are people who pour everything into their work, sometimes to the detriment of their own health—physical and/or mental. This commitment may even cost their relationships with family and friends. They can't help it. They are driven and passionate about working and hustling. Being busy is in their blood.

Then there are people that are driven more by designing their life around quality relationships and finding the beauty in "enough." For these people, time with family and friends is utterly important. Finding a nice balance between work and life is their goal.

So now we not only have employees, side hustlers, and full-on entrepreneurs, but we also have workaholics and people with a sense of balance. When we combine these various categories of people, we end up with the following possibilities:

- ✔ Workaholic employee
- ✔ Workaholic side-hustler
- ✔ Workaholic entrepreneur
- ✔ Balanced employee
- ✔ Balanced side-hustler
- ✔ Balanced entrepreneur

Can you slot yourself into one of these types?

What type of person am I? Well, I know the type I used to be before I made some changes. I started my own consulting business (www.zero-in.ca) while in my forties, when I wanted to go from employee to entrepreneur, turning from a risk-averse corporate guy who enjoyed the steady paycheck to someone that wanted to bet on myself and build something. But it also came with wanting to design a different life for myself, a more fulfilling life. Learning how to start my own business was a journey of its own.

What I didn't realize was how difficult it would be to rid myself of old habits to transform into a solopreneur and leading the life I envisioned.

This book in front of you is what I needed to read when I was first starting out on my own. Don't get me wrong, the mistakes I made turned into valuable lessons that have shaped and molded my business and me. It's not like I wasn't reading books about consulting and starting a business. But none of them seemed to apply to me and my situation. None of them talked about the life transformation I needed to go through.

It took a lot of trial and error, but I finally figured things out and got my consulting business going. I kept learning and growing and getting more clients, and I was starting to achieve that life I'd worked so hard to build by finding my niche, forcing myself to learn about networking, marketing, and sales. I figured out how to create a pipeline of new consulting clients and how to package my services. I painfully learned what types of engagements to say yes to and when to say no.

But then the pandemic hit, putting most of my consulting engagements on hold. Everything came to a crashing halt.

So, I decided to write a book: *The Zero In Formula*. A book for business leaders with strategies and tactics for how to become more customer-centric and innovative. My formula, if you will.

I learned everything I could about writing and promoting a book, and, to my surprise, it did very well. *The Zero In Formula* hit number one on Amazon in four different countries. It was then translated into Spanish and made available to a whole new audience. I was booked on over forty podcasts to talk about the book and my journey, taking my consulting business to an entirely different level.

I had suddenly increased my credibility as a consultant. I was now also an author and a sought-after speaker and an online course soon followed. The book and the course had given me some cache, and I learned the power of leveraging these new assets I had created.

Then a funny thing happened. For every person that would inquire about my consulting services, two would reach out just to ask for advice. How did I start my consulting business? How did I go about writing and marketing my book? How did I get booked as a guest on so many podcasts? How did I get featured in that article? How did I ... etc. etc.

A new opportunity presented itself. Rather than creating another book for businesses, I would write a book for people looking to take the same path as me as a solopreneur. But I needed to write a book that told the whole story. Yes, the book would include strategies and tactics around starting a business. But it also needed to speak to the heart of the matter: the great "detox" that needs to take place.

Although this book is a fictional story, it uses many elements of my own actual journey. The storyline is fictional, but the lessons are ones I learned firsthand. Some of the characters you will meet are fictionalized impersonations of real people I have encountered along the way.

So why a fictional story?

For two reasons. First, I enjoy reading a good business parable. Some of my favorite business books are told via relatable and compelling stories. They have interesting storylines and, even more, interesting characters. But the other reason is because I appreciate a good challenge. *The Zero In Formula* is a nonfiction business book, a how-to guide for business leaders. Writing that book, at the time, was a great new challenge for me. It was difficult. It tested me, and I learned a great deal. Now I needed a new challenge.

When reading the story, you will notice there are lessons and scriptural references embedded throughout. These can also be found collected together at the end of the book.

Wherever you are in your journey, you picked up this book for a reason. I hope it resonates and provides some value. If nothing else, I hope it's an interesting read.

Enjoy!

THE
PARABLE

Chapter 1

Stacy poked her head into Alex's office and asked, "Do you have an update for me yet on that partnership proposal with BlueCorp? This could be a huge win for us at DelTech."

Alex wanted to appear calm and cool in front of Stacy, as if he could handle whatever she threw his way. No, not just handle it, but knock it out of the park. Even if he was stressed on the inside, wondering how he would get this massive, complicated proposal done in such a short time frame.

"I'm making some great progress. Doing some more research on the ROI numbers we discussed including in the proposal. I'm hoping to have a first draft in your inbox by tomorrow morning."

Stacy gave Alex this to work on because she trusted him and saw him as one of her go-to leaders on the team. He always delivered. Little was she aware of the pressure she kept piling on him. But it was paying off. A promotion was at hand for Alex. Eventually, the light at the end of these killer proposals was a seat at the big table.

"You're hoping to have the first draft to me by tomorrow morning?" Stacy replied, extra sarcasm dripping off of the word "hoping."

"Not tomorrow morning. By 9:00 p.m. tonight," said Alex, who was always one to up the ante and exceed expectations. He wasn't immune to pressure. He knew this meant a day of fast food, not talking to his family, and his eyes glued to his monitor. But that's how he got to become Senior Director of Innovation at DelTech, one of the fastest growing and hottest software companies.

"That's the Alex I love. I'm counting on you. Solidifying this partnership will be a big win for us. Plus, I'd like to show the board how valuable you are to DelTech. That you would be a great fit for the open VP of Innovation role." Stacy winked and smiled at Alex as she walked away. She knew how badly he wanted that VP position. Dangling it in front of him ensured he would continue to be one of the most motivated and productive people in the company, something she had been able to rely on for the past sixteen years.

That's the Alex I love, Alex repeated in his head. *I'm counting on you.* Only, the voice in his head was much more sarcastic than Stacy's when she had said it. He loved that Stacy had confidence in him, and he loved that she was lobbying the board of directors at DelTech to promote him to the position of VP. But what a long and stressful career it had been, constantly attempting to climb the corporate ladder.

How much longer would he have to endure being strung along?

And the work itself? Alex felt like he did every time Stacy threw a new challenge his way. Conflicted. *It can't be done,* Alex thought to himself, although the lack of confidence quickly gave way to, *It will get done.*

This potential partnership with BlueCorp would allow both companies to leverage each others' technologies and innovate on a massive scale. Partnerships and proposals were neither of Alex's strengths, however. He was a software and innovation guy, and he felt in over his head on this one. Was this the one where he finally would fail to deliver? Stacy loved to challenge him, and he never turned down a chance to prove himself. The pressure was mounting.

Alex looked back at his monitor and the numbers he was crunching for the report. Then he checked his watch. 2:30 in the afternoon. He had been working on this proposal since that morning's leadership meeting. As usual, the meeting had run long and didn't finish until 12:30. When was the last time a DelTech meeting ended on time? There was always someone who felt the need to make themselves look smart. Ideas were discussed ad nauseam, decisions debated until every possible angle had been dissected. Alex had just wanted to get to work.

After being assigned this new task, Alex had gone straight from the meeting to his office to begin work on the proposal. Had he even eaten lunch yet? Did he even bring anything to eat for lunch? He'd ran out of the house so fast that morning, he had no recollection. Now, he thought he remembered his wife, Carolina, asking him, "What are you going to eat for lunch today?" Was there something both caring and accusatory in her voice? Was she suggesting he should be eating something healthy, not fast food? He couldn't be sure. Work distracted him the moment his eyes opened every morning. Oh well, he would just need to order something.

After turning his attention back to his computer and diving back into the proposal for what felt like twenty minutes, Alex checked his watch again. 5:14! Where had the time gone? Now he was starving. He dialed his go-to take out spot.

Since he missed lunch, he decided a double cheeseburger and large fries was in order. Alex didn't even have to place his order. The second they heard his voice, they knew who it was, what he liked to eat, and where to find him to bring him the food.

Calling Alex a regular was an understatement.

After hanging up, he salivated over the cholesterol rich food on its way, when his phone buzzed with an incoming text.

Where are you? Martin's game is at 7. Are you on your way home?

Martin's hockey game. His son had been asking—begging—Alex to come and watch one of his games.

They were more than halfway through the season, and Alex hadn't been to a game in months. Tonight was the night he had promised—again—saying to his son, "For sure, Buddy. Every time your skates touch the ice, I'll be screaming my head off, embarrassing you."

Alex's chest tightened as he re-read the text.

Carolina was not going to be happy. Not to mention Martin. This has been a topic of contention between Alex and Carolina for quite some time now. He could hear her saying, "Choosing work over your family. Again. Surprise, surprise."

The guilt trip. It made him feel like he was doing something wrong by working hard, providing a great living for his family.

Alex's neck and cheeks warmed, the heat working its way up to his forehead. A familiar feeling whenever the pressure built. Classic signs of stress according to an Internet search years ago when it first starting happening. Shortness of breath and lack of energy were only occasional symptoms.

He took a moment to think about how to respond to the text.

Got pulled into a big proposal. Going to be working here for a few more hours. I'll be there for the 3rd period.

Carolina's response was short, but telling.

I'm sure.

Even though it was a text, Alex read it with the same sarcasm Stacy had used earlier.

Sorry, hun.

Alex watched the three dots of Carolina replying, wondering how bad would it be.

Then the dots disappeared without a response. Was this better or worse?

Alex didn't have time to ponder it any further. Back to the proposal. Time was ticking.

It was 11:14 p.m. when Alex pulled his new Tesla into the driveway of his spacious two-story, four-bedroom house in his upscale neighbourhood. He parked in the garage and pondered what he would say to Carolina. Alex's Tesla was his pride and joy. He took an extra moment to admire it as it rested in his immaculate garage. He checked to make sure he was not overdue for a service check-up.

But Carolina. What would he say to her?

It was a Friday night or "family movie night" as they used to call it before DelTech started creeping deeper and deeper into his evenings and weekends.

Would Carolina and Martin be watching a movie?

How upset would they be that Alex had missed the hockey game?

Man, he hated that he kept letting his wife and son down. But they will be ecstatic when he soon achieved another promotion and could afford to buy them both anything they wanted.

Alex entered the house through the garage. Complete silence. No sound of a movie playing. Had they both gone to bed already?

He took off his jacket and nicely polished shoes and decided to investigate.

The family room and kitchen were both empty. No empty bowls of popcorn or chips, the two staple snacks that accompanied Friday family movie nights.

They must both be sleeping already, Alex thought to himself as he headed for the staircase, leading him upstairs to the second-floor bedrooms.

Alex was short of breath as he climbed the stairs, one at a time. Since his promotion to Senior Director of Innovation, and the workday going from eight to twelve hours, Alex had little time for a healthy lifestyle. He hadn't exercised in months, maybe years. The steady diet of fast food for lunch and dinner didn't help. He had time to only work and sleep. Rinse and repeat.

In a few more months, once he was VP of Innovation, he would have more time again, and then he could devote himself to eating healthy and getting back in shape. For now, Alex would try to not get past being forty pounds overweight. Climbing the stairs to his second-floor bedroom, which was proving to be more of a challenge as each week passed, would have to suffice as his daily exercise.

Alex arrived at the landing of the second floor thoroughly out of breath. After taking a few seconds to recover, he tiptoed towards Martin's room. Peeking his head in the door, he found his son fast asleep. His bedroom walls, decorated with posters of his favorite hockey players, reminded Alex of his younger self. A great hockey player during his own teenage years, Alex loved the game. He had every intention of being very involved in Martin's teams. Assistant coach, perhaps even head coach. Maybe next year. Maybe once he got the promotion.

After closing the door to Martin's room, his next stop was the master bedroom, where he was hoping to find Carolina asleep, as well. Earlier in their marriage, they would stay up talking for hours on a Friday night, sharing the ups and downs of their weeks with each other, discussing hopes and dreams for the next twenty years of their lives together, never taking for granted their open communication, which they both understood was the foundation of a great marriage.

But tonight, with Alex coming home late again after working on yet another important project for DelTech, no communication with Carolina would make things much easier on him.

Alex opened the door and found Carolina sound asleep, her back turned to him as she lay in bed. Alex breathed a deep sigh of relief. Tomorrow, he would explain to her the importance of the BlueCorp partnership and how it would set him up for the VP role.

After preparing for bed, Alex was careful to slowly and quietly pull back the covers, careful not to disturb his wife. As he was about to climb into bed, he noticed a piece of paper on his pillow. A note from Carolina.

My love, can we please take some time to talk tomorrow?

Short. Simple. But what did she want to talk about? Alex pondered this as he slipped under the covers. He let his mind unwind from his whirlwind week of constant high-pressure meetings and short deadlines. As he lay there, he thought of the proposal he had sent to Stacy an hour earlier. Had he covered everything that needed to be addressed, gotten all the main points across? Were his ROI calculations accurate?

As his mind raced, he thought of at least half-a-dozen new ideas for the proposal. He must write them down. Alex reached for the pen on his bedside table and jotted down his thoughts on the back of the same sheet of paper Carolina used for the note she'd left on his pillow.

Feeling like his mind was finally at ease, Alex drifted off to sleep. He would update the proposal first thing in the morning and impress Stacy with these additional ideas.

Saturday morning broke with Alex waking up to the sound of silence in the still house. It was 6:30 a.m. and he was wide awake, his mind racing with thoughts about the proposal. Carolina and Martin were both still sleeping.

He'd take the next hour to update the proposal, get it off to Stacy, and have the rest of the day for some quality time with my family, Alex thought to himself.

He quietly got dressed and slipped downstairs to the kitchen where he put on a pot of coffee. With long days, short nights, and tons of work to do, coffee had become his savior and fuel. He was up to four or five cups a day.

With a fresh cup in hand, he went to log onto his computer and get to work. His home office had become a place where he was spending a lot of time on weekends the past few years. Last year, he and Carolina even took a one-week staycation. Yet rather than the nature hikes, kayaking, and hanging out in the local cafes like they had planned, Alex spent the majority of that week in this office working.

But today Alex would have the proposal updated and sent off before Carolina and Martin were awake. They would have no idea he had been up working.

Alex checked his email and was surprised to see a response from Stacy to his proposal. Her email had come in at 2:38 a.m. She had read the proposal and given her feedback. A lot of feedback. On top of the six or seven ideas Alex had already planned to add to the document, Stacy had identified fifteen more changes to include. Did she have a life outside work?

Slumping back in his chair with his shoulders drooping, Alex felt deflated. These updates would take him hours. He had to research, crunch more numbers, and wordsmith some value points into the proposal. In her email, Stacy asked for the updates by Monday morning. But Alex, always looking to exceed expectations, set a goal to have it back to her by noon today. This way he'd still be able to have quality time with his family.

He took a long, slow sip from his coffee, rolled up his sleeves, and got to work.

At 8:11 a.m., Martin came downstairs and into the kitchen. Cupboard doors opened and closed. Dishes and pots banged against each other and the counter. Another cabinet door slammed shut. Then the fridge door opened and closed. Alex was finding it difficult to concentrate with all this movement and noise. He could hear the flakes of cereal settling into the bowl, and then the milk being poured, some landing on the counter, an irritated grunt coming from his kid.

"Can you keep it down in there? I'm trying to get some work done," Alex called out to Martin.

"Good morning, Dad. You should have seen me last night. A goal and three assists. We won 5-3. What a game!" Martin added. The excitement in his voice was palpable. He was sharing his personal and team accomplishments with his dad, his hockey hero.

Martin was talking much too loud for Alex's liking. The update about Martin's game was more annoying than exciting. He was trying to concentrate on his proposal. But he feigned enthusiasm in return, hoping it would appease Martin and end the conversation. He did want to hear all about the game, but first he needed a few more hours to finish the report.

"Dad, too bad you didn't make it. What happened? You said you were for sure going to come. My best game of the season, I'm telling you," Martin said, walking into Alex's office.

Is this worth it? Alex thought to himself briefly. *Here I am, sitting in my home office on a Saturday morning, absorbed in work, annoyed that my son wants to talk to me about his hockey game.*

Alex shook off those thoughts. *Let me just get through the next few months, move into the VP position, and then I can slow down and make more time for family. For now, don't get distracted. If I take the foot off the gas now, I may not get the promotion. I'd be stuck writing more proposals on my weekends.* Alex continued to think to himself. He needed to respond to Martin and buy himself some time.

"Sorry, buddy. I planned on being there, but something super important came up at work. In fact, I am just trying to finish it now. Why don't you go have your cereal and watch something on Netflix? This afternoon, you can tell me all about your game." Alex was pleased with the patience and consideration of his response. Even if Martin's shoulders slumped.

He retreated to the family room to eat his breakfast on the couch and turned on the TV, a little louder than Alex would have liked. "Turn it down!" Alex screamed from the office.

Carolina sauntered lazily down the stairs and slowly entered the kitchen, rubbing her eyes. To say she was not a morning person would be stating the obvious. Born and raised in Chile, she was used to a slow and relaxed lifestyle.

Up until the age of twenty-three, her life consisted of regular afternoon siestas, late night meals, and lots of time with family. Those were her staples growing up. Her parents had a rock-solid marriage with her father working over forty years in the mining industry as a top-notch metallurgist. Her mother stayed home to raise the kids and was a loving and supportive partner. Carolina appreciated her father's work ethic and dedication to his career. She also held great admiration her mother's caring and compassionate nature. After college, she moved away to travel and experience life in other parts of the world. That's when she'd met Alex.

He loved that she was from South America, was fluent in both Spanish and English, beautiful, kind, generous, and had an accent to die for. Carolina loved that Alex was passionate, hard working, sensitive, and dedicated. They had a whirlwind romance, dating for a year and half before getting married. Everything about their life and marriage had been complete bliss for several years. But this new "hustle culture" lifestyle Alex had adopted since his last promotion was definitely not something she had signed up for.

She poured herself a cup of coffee and headed to the living room.

"Why are you eating your cereal on the couch with the TV on?" Alex could hear his wife's frustrated voice asking Martin.

"Dad told me to. I was trying to tell him about my hockey game last night, but he was too busy with work stuff."

Carolina stomped into the office. Alex's eyes were glued to monitor as he crunched numbers.

"Working still?" she said in an exasperated voice. "It's Saturday!"

"This proposal is a big one. I thought I had it done last night, but then Stacy already ripped it apart and asked me to make a million changes."

Alex conveniently left out the part about how he got up early, intending to update the proposal.

"Is that the note I left you last night?" Carolina pointed to the piece of paper sitting on Alex's desk.

"Yes, I got it. We'll have lots of time to talk later, I promise," Alex replied. "Let me get this in by noon and then I'm all yours."

She turned and left the office, asking Martin to turn off the TV and eat his breakfast at the kitchen table, where she joined him. They made plans for some fun mother and son time and then headed out. Alex never even heard the front door close.

By noon, Alex was starving. The proposal was going to take several more hours to finish. But he needed some fuel.

"Honey, what are we doing for lunch?" he called out, to no one.

It finally dawned on him that he had been alone in the house, for hours. Carolina and Martin must have left at some point when he was deep into his work.

Annoyed he would have to get up and make himself something to eat, but with little time to spare, he headed to the freezer, where he grabbed a box of frozen pizza pockets, the kind that takes only three minutes in the microwave. Starving, he took out three from the box.

After scarfing down this completely unhealthy lunch over the sink, Alex headed back to his computer, back to DelTech, back to his ticket for a promotion to VP of Innovation.

When he returned his desk, his eyes seized on the note Carolina had left on his pillow the night before.

My love, can we please take some time to talk tomorrow?

Alex looked at his watch. It was now 12:24 and he had only shared a couple of short and unpleasant words with Carolina so far that morning. He felt an instant pang of guilt and remorse. His wife, who had been so supportive of him over the years, was asking for some time with him, and all he did was brush her off.

He checked his phone to see if Carolina had texted him. Nothing.

What choice did he have now but to plow through and get the proposal done, so he could devote Saturday night to time with his family.

At 3:47, Alex finally finished the second draft of the proposal. What should have brought relief instead caused panic, as he immediately began to consider what Stacy would think of the updates. Other questions filtered into his head.

How mad was Carolina?

What should he do to make it up to Martin?

Alex hit send on the email and then got up from his chair. With his head sweaty and spinning, he felt even more lethargic than usual. Now, just getting out of his chair seemed like a challenge.

He stretched his arms high over is head.

He was forty-one years old and forty pounds overweight.

He felt like he was seventy. Both of his knees and his back ached. He could barely stand up straight without feeling like every muscle in his body was screaming at him.

Alex showered and changed out of his pajama pants and t-shirt. After slipping into a nice pair of jeans and a button-up shirt, he felt a little better.

He grabbed his phone and called Carolina's cell. No answer.

Alex left a voice message. "Hi, honey, great news. My proposal is finished, and we now have the rest of the weekend for downtime. What should we do for dinner? And let's take that time to talk tonight like you asked. Love you."

Alex was pleased with himself. The rest of the weekend would give him lots of time to make up for his actions of Friday night and Saturday morning.

Carolina and Martin returned home just before five. Alex was waiting for them and happy to hear all about Martin's hockey game from the night before.

Carolina was tired from a busy week of running Martin to and from school and hockey, cooking, laundry, and taking care of the house. She did not work outside of the home, but with Alex's busy schedule and Martin's school and extracurricular activities, she took care of everything family and house related.

They decided to order in pizza for dinner. For Carolina and Martin, this would be a nice treat. For Alex, this would be his fifth take-out dinner in the last seven days. He was hoping for a home cooked meal, but was always happy to feed his growing addiction to greasy food.

After dinner, Martin went to visit his friend Mateo two houses over. They were close friends and spent a lot of time at each other's house. Martin was to be home by nine, which would give Alex and Carolina time to talk.

Before sitting down on the couch, Alex stole a peek at his phone. Another email from Stacy!

He scanned it quickly and saw she was quite happy with the latest draft. But she still had several changes for Alex to make before Monday. His breath started to labour and his chest tightened at the thought of the work.

Alex did not let Carolina know about the email. He decided he better keep it to himself, at least, for now. He had promised his wife his time and attention for the rest of the weekend. Now his boss had stolen it away, again. How was he going to handle this? Thanks a lot, Stacy.

They sat on the couch and Carolina bared her feelings. She let her husband know how much she missed their talks and how both she and Martin were both feeling second best. With Alex, DelTech came first and his family was suffering. His health was suffering. He was, she believed, a workaholic.

Deep down, he knew she was right about a lot of things. But that's not what he told her. Instead, Alex's defensive instincts kicked in.

"I work hard to provide. So that we can have this nice house. So you don't have to work and Martin can play hockey and we can save for our retirement. That's not easy, and my job is very demanding. You used to be so supportive of me. What happened?"

Like that, Alex had painted Carolina as the villain and made himself into the victim. Not a great move. He used to be empathetic, a great listener. Now he was defensive and short-tempered. He didn't like the person he had become. But was it his fault? He was just trying to provide for his family and now he was being attacked.

After some back and forth bickering, Carolina retreated to the bedroom to be alone, to be away from Alex.

Alex took the opportunity to head into his office and read Stacy's email again and assess the situation. This would be another few hours of work on Sunday. He could get it done in the afternoon after they were home from church and had lunch. This was doable.

Again, Alex's eyes went to the note on his desk.

My love, can we please take some time to talk tomorrow?

That talk had just happened and it didn't go well. What had he done? Had he spoken to her too harshly? A brief moment of regret soon turned into a prolonged feeling of defiance. Had he really done anything wrong? Why was she angry with him? Why couldn't she understand his position? He could feel his skin turning red as the warm feeling returned to his cheeks. Alex felt overwhelmed, felt pressure coming from every corner in his life. To top it all off, the tightening in his chest came back.

Breathe, he told himself. *Deep breath in. Deep breath out. You got this.*

Work was becoming too much. Could he handle it?

His relationship with Carolina was fraying. Could he repair it?

His son was dying to have his dad's attention. Could he give it to him?

More deep breaths.

The sound of Martin returning home brought Alex's thoughts back to the present. He looked at the computer screen. The proposal was waiting. He turned to see Martin walking into the house. A glance back at the computer.

Alex decided to reach forward and power down his laptop. The proposal could wait until tomorrow. Now was his opportunity to spend some time with Martin.

He left his office and welcomed Martin back home from his visit with Mateo. They spent the next hour chatting about hockey. They talked about last night's game. They talked about the team. They talked about Martin's wrist shot and how fast and accurate it was becoming. Martin was all smiles after their chat as he went off to brush his teeth and get ready for bed.

But truthfully, Alex was not fully present. All he could think about was the proposal, and whether he should fight through his exhaustion and start working on it. If he got it done now, that would free up his Sunday.

After putting Martin to bed, he decided to head downstairs to relax on the couch in front of the TV. He would take a few minutes to watch something before heading back to his office and the proposal. Once he picked a movie to watch, he sprawled out on the couch and soon nodded off. Alex was famous for seeing the first five minutes of many movies.

Sunday morning broke with Carolina waking Alex with a nudge of the shoulder and a gentle reminder that they had to get ready for church.

The entire morning was a blur. Sitting in church pew, Alex scarcely heard a word of Pastor Johnson's sermon. Not that it was dry or boring. Quite the opposite. Marcus Johnson was a gifted speaker, who always brought so much insight to his Sunday morning sermons. But Alex's mind was on his proposal. He tuned in and out of the sermon, picking up pieces here and there as Pastor Johnson talked about some of King Solomon's insights in the book Ecclesiastes.

"Whoever loves money never has enough; whoever loves wealth is never satisfied with their income."

Carolina, nodding her head in agreement with the message, took careful notes as she glanced at Alex, who was barely paying attention.

Pastor Johnson quoted the Apostle Paul from the book of 1 Timothy, "For the love of money is a root of all kinds of evil."

Carolina again nodded as Alex daydreamed. While his thoughts should have been in the present moment, all he could think about was the future. Being the VP of Innovation. Making even more money, wearing even nicer clothes, driving an even fancier Tesla. Or would he keep his current Tesla and buy a second one in a different color? He would be the envy of so many people.

Then came a quote from Jesus himself from the book of Matthew.

"No one can serve two masters. Either you will hate the one and love the other, or you will be devoted to the one and despise the other. You cannot serve both God and money."

Alex received a look from Carolina that indicated she was convinced the lifestyle he was chasing was misguided; his priorities misaligned.

Meanwhile, Alex had figured out a way to present some of the points Stacy was asking for in the report. He caught some of Pastor Johnson's message but completely missed any context.

After lunch, Alex rushed to his home office to finish the proposal. Again, it took longer than he anticipated. In the evening, Carolina made a home cooked dinner of salmon with rice, dumplings, and asparagus. Alex, with no time to spare, ate at his desk.

That next morning, on his drive into work, Alex listened to a podcast where the host and guest were discussing a university study about how much money people actually need to live a happy life. The study found that our overall well-being does rise with our income but only to a point. At a certain point, one either plateaus, or, worse, one's level of happiness declines. Our emotional well-being is as good as it's going to get with an income of around $100,000. Beyond that point, money will not make our lives better. The study mentioned that $100,000 is an approximate number, depending on where you live, cost of living, etc. But the point was clear.

$100,000? That's it? I make way more than that already! Alex thought to himself. *And I'm far from happy. Wait, am I happy?* He'd never stopped to consider the question. Alex's salary was $165,000.

He had already surpassed the point where no amount of money was going to increase his well-being and happiness.

By societal standards, Alex was extremely successful. A high-paying job at a successful company. A nice house, nice car. Married with a son.

He had lots of expensive toys, but little time to enjoy them. He had a wonderful wife, who was currently not talking to him. His son idolized him and wanted to follow in his footsteps as a hockey player, but Alex barely made time to watch him play. He even shooed him out of his office the other day when he tried to talk to Alex about his game.

The one thing Alex should be looking forward to was the strategic planning session happening later that afternoon. Those types of collective brainstorming sessions would typically energize him. Dissecting the company's strengths, weaknesses, opportunities, and threats. Pitching creative new ideas to move the business to the next level. Alex used to love those types of meetings, but in the past the past few years, DelTech started bringing in outside consultants to facilitate these strategy sessions. Needing an outside perspective was the reasoning. This was a theme Alex would see more of in the coming months.

Now, just thinking about today's strategy planning session was adding to Alex's stress. To be fair, he enjoyed the facilitated discussions, often daydreaming that it was him leading the leadership team through similar sessions. But he also felt a bit miffed when his coworkers would hang on every word the consultants would say as if their ideas were new and revolutionary.

Sometimes they brought fresh new perspectives, but, other times, they would state opinions and bring ideas that were almost exact copies of something Alex had brought up in a leadership meeting only weeks earlier, the only difference being that everyone listened to the consultant and showed a willingness to dive deeper into their ideas. Alex always felt slighted when a similar idea he had voiced was summarily dismissed because "it would never work" or "we have tried something like that before without success." Stacy had actually used both of those lines with Alex during last year's strategy session.

Alex wondered what it might feel like to sit on the other side of the table. To be the consultant. To be seen as the expert with great ideas.

At the thought of today's strategy meeting, Alex's chest tightened. This time it felt worse than usual.

Luckily, he was now pulling into the parking lot at DelTech, his breathing laboured. Alex felt anxious and overwhelmed. Was he taking on too much at work? Was it robbing him of a happy marriage? Was he missing out on quality time with his son? Was he even happy? Was the promotion the answer to all his problems?

He took a deep breath and got out of his car slowly, his head spinning. As he stood, he supported himself with one hand on the open car door. Ahead of him would be another insane day of useless meetings, tight deadlines, a barrage of endless emails, and new pressures from Stacy. At home, a family he was neglecting.

It was as if each new overwhelming thought drained more of his energy. There was no strength in any muscle of his body. Another deep breath. His head began to spin faster.

The last image he remembered was Rob Langley pulling into the parking spot next to him, Rob getting out of his car, and, with a smug smirk on his face, looking at Alex and saying, "Hey, Alex, happy Monday. You finally ready to lose to me in squash?"

Rob, who was in great shape and a superb squash player, knew Alex was out of shape and liked to rub it in. He had been chiding Alex for months about playing against each other. Alex didn't have the time or the energy to play squash against Rob. If he did, he would want to win so badly and put Rob in his place.

No, Alex had meetings and deadlines and reports and proposals piling up. He had no time for squash. He barely had time to breathe. When he was breathing, it was labored. How could he get through all of these responsibilities and finally lighten his load?

Alex's chest tightened further, and then his mind went blank.

CHAPTER REFLECTION QUESTIONS

- ✔ Have you ever found yourself in a work situation similar to Alex's?
- ✔ Would you consider yourself a workaholic?
- ✔ How does it impact relationships with family and friends if you consistently prioritize work ahead of them?
- ✔ What are you doing to ensure your health is not neglected due to your work?

Chapter 2

It was 10:43 p.m. when Alex pulled into the driveway of his dark and quiet house. As usual, Martin and Carolina had already gone to bed. Had he even seen either of them that day? When was the last time he saw them? He had been leaving early every morning in a rush and coming home late exhausted.

As he walked through the door, preparing himself to trudge up the stairs to his bedroom, Alex stopped himself cold, his eyes fixing on a family photo hanging on the wall. The picture was taken while on vacation at a cottage five years ago. The photo showed Alex, easily forty pounds lighter, smiling because he had just spent several consecutive days relaxing with Carolina, teaching Martin how to fish. Carolina looked as beautiful as ever. She held Alex's hand in the picture, her other arm wrapped around Martin's shoulder. Martin was eight at the time. The look on his face indicated a happy childhood. Alex vividly remembered that vacation.

And yet here he was, now two months removed from his incident in the parking lot at work. His mind shot back to that day.

He could still hear Carolina's voice echoing in his ear when he woke up groggy in the hospital. "The doctor says you had a panic attack. You had us scared, Alex. At first, they thought it was a heart attack," Carolina had informed him. "Rob saw you collapse in the parking lot at work and called the ambulance."

And yet, all Alex could think about that day, while lying in the hospital bed, was work. Even though he had just been informed about his panic attack. Even though for nine hours he was monitored by nurses and doctors who took turns checking his heart rate and blood pressure and ran tests on his blood. Even though he was being advised how he would need to eat healthier, slow down at work, and start taking an anti-anxiety medication he couldn't pronounce. It was DelTech that consumed his thoughts that day.

It wasn't until he got home and settled into the couch that night that he remembered to check his phone.

There were several text messages and emails and one voice message waiting for him. He had listened to the voice message first. It was from Stacy.

"Hi, Alex, I heard about your issue this morning. We were all worried when you didn't show up for the leadership meeting. Rob says it sounds like you had some kind of indigestion or something? Better watch what you're eating. We need you back here pronto. Great job on the BlueCorp proposal. I sent it on to their VP of Partnerships today and am already hearing some great things back from them. You might have just won us that deal. The VP position is looking good! Listen, when you're back in the office tomorrow, come and see me first thing. I want to talk to you about another project I would like you to lead. This one is going to make the BlueCorp proposal look like chump change."

Did Stacy not even care about his health? She seemed to dismiss it as if it was nothing. And did the BlueCorp proposal really bring him another step closer to the VP position? Or did it just earn him more high-pressure work on his plate, making his life even busier than it already was? Would the rat race ever end? These were rhetorical questions, as he found himself coming home late from work, again.

A glance back to the family photo.

Where have the last five years gone? Alex thought to himself—the walks with Carolina as they held hands, the father and son time with Martin, solidifying his role as Martin's hero, the barbequed meals, and time around the campfire roasting marshmallows. Was that their last relaxing vacation away together as a family?

Alex got his start at DelTech when he was a fresh-faced software developer and there were only eighty-seven people in the company. He quickly established himself as a top-notch coder, one who was driven, smart, and dedicated. He soon started climbing the ranks, first with a promotion to team lead. A few years later, they gave him the role of manager. Then he became a director, before finally settling into his role of senior director.

His first few years at the company had been fun. The team building events, the company scavenger hunts, the Christmas parties. For Alex it became his home away from home.

But with each promotion, the pressure escalated, and Alex was further removed from his love of coding complex algorithms. Software challenges were replaced by leadership, strategy, and broader innovation challenges. The goal posts were set further down the field. In order for Alex to continue to climb to the next step on the corporate ladder, he would face increasing responsibilities. The fun times seemed like a fading object in his rearview mirror.

DelTech, in its current state, now boasted over a thousand employees. Alex had been a part of a lot of hard work and growth in the past sixteen years. Where was all this stress and pressure leading? It seemed to only increase without an end in sight.

After some fond memories and tearful reflections, Alex finally made his way upstairs. He caught his breath and checked on Martin, who was sound asleep. Next, he would quietly slip in to bed and not disturb Carolina. He did not want to wake his wife. She would likely be ready to remind him about his panic attack from a few months ago, cautioning him that he had again taken on too much at work. She stressed to him that his son was still dying to have his dad come watch even one of his hockey games.

It had been two months since the panic attack, and, apparently, Alex had not learned anything from the experience.

Stacy wasn't kidding when she had said that this next challenge for Alex was a game changer for DelTech. The BlueCorp partnership was looking good. Everyone was pleased with what Alex had proposed. If the two companies could work well together, it would account for an extra 15% of revenue for DelTech.

But the new project Alex was leading with SlickPay was massive by comparison. DelTech had been trying for years to break into a completely new vertical, and SlickPay was their golden ticket.

"Amazon started out as an online book store and then expanded into a global online marketplace for just about any product," was the line Alex kept hearing from Stacy.

Now that DelTech was already a major player in the enterprise software space, it was time for them to diversify and take on the direct-to-consumer technology sector. The pressure was on him to help turn them into the next Amazon.

A major part of this plan was SlickPay, a small software company that was growing their user base at a rapid pace, and one that DelTech has recently purchased. The young founders were more than happy to sell the business and take the payout. Alex was the guy to lead a team that would enhance and scale the product even further.

The early projections suggested that it could increase revenue by another 45% if they played their cards right. The realization of this growth would be resting primarily on Alex's shoulders.

"With your skills, background, and track record, you're a natural pick to lead this new venture," was how Stacy had pitched it to him. It was half flattery, half passive-aggressive motivation. It seemed like a double-edged sword to Alex. "The board will be eager to see the results," as if Alex needed help seeing the carrot dangling in front of him.

This new project was not something that would overtake his life for just a few days, like the BlueCorp proposal. This project would be months of pressure-filled days chained to his desk. Would Alex see any of Martin's hockey games this season?

How many more notes would Carolina have to leave on his pillow? She was a supportive and loving wife like her mother had always been to her father. But everyone has their limits. Was he pushing Carolina past hers?

Would his stress and anxiety levels stay in check? Or would he find himself experiencing another panic attack, or worse?

Alex brushed off these thoughts and focused his attention back on work. Over the next few weeks, he found himself buried in meetings.

Meetings to discuss what his software developers were finding as they reviewed the SlickPay code.

Meetings to plan how they would eventually pilot and test their new and improved version of the product.

Meetings about how to potentially brand, market, and sell their new direct-to-consumer application.

Meetings with the wider innovation teams to ensure everyone was on track with each of their projects.

Meetings with individuals on his team to make sure he was investing in them and their career paths.

Alex could feel himself getting stressed about everything that lay ahead of him: the pressure, the timelines, the expectations.

Not to mention the meetings with Stacy to keep her up to date on everything. He knew Stacy hated surprises. She needed to know every detail, and he catered to this need.

Carolina had been asking for a time the two of them could meet for lunch. Alex desperately wanted to have a lunch date with his wife. At a minimum, he wanted to at least stop letting her down. Yet, looking at his calendar, he could not find even a fifteen-minute timeslot on any day of the week. Things had ramped up to a torrid pace for Alex. But he was doing a masterful job of juggling all of these responsibilities and keeping everything on track. At work, at least.

Things were moving along nicely with SlickPay; however, it would be months before the first pilot project would be ready to roll out.

Until then, the take-out meals would pile up, Alex's waistline would continue to expand, he would take his anxiety medication—whenever he remembered— and his relationships with his wife and son would take a back seat to everything.

One night, Alex came home late again from work with what felt like the weight of the world on his shoulders.

To his surprise, a lamp was on the master bedroom. Carolina was not asleep. She had stayed up waiting for Alex.

"I know what you're going to say," Alex said, trying to preempt the conversation, hand held up as if to stop an anticipated attack from his wife. "I'm late again."

"Alex, come here," Carolina replied softly, patting his spot on the bed. It was a gentle invitation for him to come sit next to her.

The tension in Alex's shoulders eased as he realized she was not angry, like he had been expecting. He sat beside her on the bed, and she took hold of his hand.

"Honey, I miss you," she said in a quiet voice as she looked in his eyes. Alex's cheeks felt warm, but it was not a reaction to the typical stress he had been feeling. This time it was due to the love he felt from and for his wife.

"You know I am proud of you and everything you have accomplished," she continued in her soft Chilean accent. "But when is it enough? When will you see that we don't need anything more? More money is not going to make us any happier. A more expensive house or car won't make me any prouder of you. More promotions at work aren't going to make you a better father to Martin. The only thing we need more of is *you*."

That last line hit home like a dagger through his heart. Alex knew deep down he had been neglecting his family. Suddenly, there was clarity. The path he was on at DelTech was not going to lead him to what he truly wanted in life, which was to leave a legacy as a great husband and father. But he was knee-deep into this major project and the VP position was within his grasp. He just had to press a little bit further. Besides, he was providing for his family. Wasn't that a good legacy to leave? Wasn't that what good husbands and fathers did?

"Carolina, I realize I have been working way too much. But it will all slow down soon. I'm so close to realizing the perfect situation," Alex replied. He almost believed it himself. Almost.

"Will things slow down? That is what you thought after the BlueCorp proposal. And now look. You're even busier than you were then." Carolina's voice was filled with equal parts empathy and frustration.

"What should I do, quit my job?" Alex shot back, his voice dripping with defensiveness.

"Take an afternoon off. Let's do something together. Like we used to. Some quality time."

"I would love that, Carolina, but I can't even find time to breathe. How can I possibly take off an entire afternoon?"

"Don't you think that's a problem?"

Alex let that sink in. That was a problem. And he knew it. They continued to talk more about his need to slow down, and the conversation ended with him finally agreeing to take an afternoon off. Next week, he would spend a day relaxing at the spa with his patient and compassionate wife.

On one hand, it relieved Alex to know he had quality time planned with Carolina. In some ways, having time off was great. Time to relax, unwind, spend time with family and friends. Time to think about anything but work. Time for Alex to be a husband, father, and friend. Time for Alex to be Alex.

Yet, he worried that even those few hours away from the office would result in more work piling up on his plate. He couldn't even think about a week's vacation. With each day off, more work would pile up.

More emails waiting in his inbox. More critical decisions to make. More fires to put out. Would Alex even be able to relax if he was to take a vacation? Or would his mind become even more overwhelmed? Would he worry about everything that would be waiting for him at DelTech when he returned?

For now, he would settle for an afternoon off with his wife. That was about all he could afford at the moment.

That Sunday, Alex found himself paying a little more attention to Pastor Johnson's sermon, whose main theme was about our short time in this earthly life and understanding the importance of how we spend it.

"'So, teach us to number our days that we may we get a heart of wisdom,'" he read from Psalm 90. Wise words from Moses himself.

Do I appreciate that my time is limited? Am I spending my days wisely? Alex pondered. *I am forty-one years old. These are prime years for me to be creating a more solid foundation for my marriage with Carolina, but what foundation am I laying?* Alex took a deep

Chapter 2

THE PARABLE

breath and squirmed in his seat as he wrestled with this question. *This is also time I should be using to set a great example for Martin as he grows into a young man. Am I setting the right example for him?* More uncomfortable questions.

Another deep breath.

But I work hard, make great money, and provide for my family, Alex was reasoning with himself now. *Maybe I am spending my time wisely.* Now he was trying to convince himself. More deep breaths. More to think about, later, after he completed the SlickPay project.

When Alex arrived at work on Monday morning, Stacy was waiting for him in his office.

"Come on in and close the door. I have a few things to share with you," she said, an uncomfortable look on her face.

Alex was not sure what to think. "Okay," was his response as he stepped into his office and slowly closed the door behind him.

"First, let me congratulate you on all the great work you and the team are doing on the SlickPay project."

Start by buttering me up, Alex thought to himself. *Here comes the bad news.* He had seen this technique from her many times before. When Stacy joined DelTech over twenty years ago, she was fresh out of school and rough around the edges.

She was brilliant and had a great work ethic to go along with her passion, but the soft skills were lacking. Now, at fifty, she was a master at controlling the communication and the message. It came from her years of difficult negotiations. Plus, years of on-the-job mentoring coupled with corporate training. DelTech had invested a lot in her and her career over the years, and it showed. She was smooth. But it came with a price.

Eight years ago, Stacy's husband decided he had played second fiddle to her career long enough. After coming home from work late one night, Stacy walked into a house with half the furniture gone and a note informing her the marriage was over. Of course, she was devasted. Alex had a front row seat to the wide range of emotions she'd experienced, including many discussions in their one-on-one meetings about her various regrets. Yet, rather than causing her to pull back on her work and finding a more balanced life for herself, it caused her to dive even deeper into her career. It was the one thing she had left. It was her identity.

The one good thing that came out of that dark time was a new closeness that formed between Alex and Stacy. She had opened up to him. He was a great listener and provided the ear she needed at the time.

"But I need to let you know about some conversations happening at the board level," Stacy started. "They believe that in order to take DelTech to the next level, it might be in the company's best interest to hire someone with an outsider perspective for the VP of Innovation role."

And there it was. Like a nail through his heart. Alex's shoulders dropped. He closed his eyes and took a deep breath.

Stacy observed his body language and tried to soften the blow. "These are just conversations," she added. "It doesn't mean it's a final decision. I am continuing to keep them up to date on the great work you are doing and reminding them we need to reward people like you who have gotten us to where we are today. Keep doing what you are doing and have faith it will cement your case."

By now, Stacy's voice was just background noise. All Alex could think about was how he had been neglecting Carolina and Martin for the past several years in pursuit of the elusive VP position, the golden egg he believed would be his ticket to a life of financial freedom and fulfillment. Was climbing the corporate ladder really the road to the life he dreamt about? Or was it actually holding him back from being the husband and father he desperately wanted to be?

Alex sleepwalked through the rest of the work day half resentful, half embarrassed. The resentment was towards Stacy, the board, and DelTech, in general. He was embarrassed just thinking about how much he had been deprioritizing time with the people most important to him. He felt like a fool, a sucker.

✦ ✦ ✦

When he gave Carolina the news that evening, she was incredibly empathetic and supportive, like she had always been.

"Oh, Alex, that must have been so devastating for you." She wrapped her arms around him, her warm hug helping to relieve the sting of the situation. Alex recognized she was a much better partner to him than he had been to her.

That evening, after Martin went to bed, Alex and Carolina spent several hours talking, much like they used to. They talked about their hopes and wishes, imagining places they would love to visit, dreaming of experiences they would like to give Martin. It was great to feel connected to his wife again.

For the next three days, Alex actually felt a little more energized at work. He was moving meetings along more quickly. Action items were getting accomplished. Emails were read and answered promptly. Reports were written and delivered with a little more zeal than usual. Alex knew he had an afternoon at the spa with Carolina coming up, and although he was still holding out hope for the elusive VP position, his excitement came from the idea of spending some much needed quality time with his wife. If he could get ahead of his work, he could relax and enjoy his time with Carolina.

The meetings, emails, and deadlines still continued at a chaotic pace. Alex put in long hours and was working like crazy. By the time lunch on Thursday rolled around, he was still knee-deep in unfinished work. But he shut down his laptop and left to pick up Carolina for their afternoon date. Would he have dared taken time off during a busy period a few short months ago? Something was changing inside Alex. But what was it exactly? Was it mere resignation over the thought of losing the promotion, or was it something deeper?

"Mr. and Mrs. Green," the young lady at the reception smiled and greeted them as they entered the spa. "We are so happy to have you again. I see it has been a few years since your last visit. Great to have you back."

Indoor pools, outdoor pools, and hot tubs. Steam rooms, reading rooms, games rooms, yoga rooms, and tea rooms. Traditional European massages, Swedish massages, hot stone massages, and aromatherapy.

This was no ordinary spa. This was luxury and relaxation combined and bottled into a sumptuous and romantic setting.

For the next three hours, Alex and Carolina were pampered. They felt like royalty as their minds and bodies were treated to a variety of smells, sounds, and other wonderful sensations.

"Is it just me or does this coffee taste so much better than what we drink at home," Alex pondered out loud during their afternoon high tea sitting. He savored each sip, eyes closed, an attempt to relish in the moment even more.

"This is actually the same brand we drink at home," Carolina informed him.

"You know, I can explain the taste difference. There's this study I heard about that if you drink the exact same coffee in two drastically different environments, your perception of the taste will be different. A high-quality cup of in a loud and busy greasy spoon restaurant served in an ordinary mug will taste just okay. But that same cup of coffee served in a relaxing setting with beautiful surroundings, poured in a fancy cup, and served with a napkin in your favorite color is going to taste amazing," Alex explained.

"That makes sense," Carolina responded. "I guess it is safe to say you are enjoying your surroundings then?"

"Yes, it is very safe to say that."

During his massage, Alex was sure he actually fell asleep on the table at one point. His body relaxed and his mind no longer filled with thoughts of projects and meetings, he remembered what it felt like to live in the moment again.

He came out of the massage with all the tension from his neck and shoulders gone. So used to carrying around that much stress, it was like he had forgotten what it felt like to not have it. A weight lifted. A burden removed.

The time in the hot tub only relaxed his muscles and mind even more. It sure didn't hurt that he was in a romantic setting with his beautiful wife, something that had not happened in a long time. Too long.

"Why did it take me so long to do something like that with you?" he asked Carolina on the drive home. "This is the first time I can remember in well ... forever where I haven't been completely consumed by all things DelTech."

Caroline smiled at him and held his hand as they drove home together. This was how their time together was meant to be. Engaged, connected, in tune with one another.

Alex finally checked his phone later that evening to discover, as expected, a long string of emails in his inbox. He first read through the ones that seemed most important, responding to the ones where he could give quick input and keep projects moving. Alex hated the feeling of being a bottleneck. But there were so many emails.

Emails asking for his opinion.

Emails giving him updates.

Emails he was copied on and had no idea why.

Emails upon emails.

Within minutes, Alex's neck and shoulders tensed

up. Gone were the loose muscles that had been massaged and relaxed at the spa. Back was the work stress. He reached for the bag of chips in his desk drawer out of instinct. His eyes searched the room for his bottle of Coke, like a detective looking for clues at the scene of a crime. Back were Alex's old habits and coping mechanisms. Back as easily as they had left.

But it was the last email Alex read that got his skin turning red. An announcement to everyone in the company about Rob Langley's promotion to Associate VP of Business Development. The email detailed the great work Rob had done at DelTech over the years and asked everyone to help congratulate him on his new role. Response after response offering praise and congratulations poured in from people around the company.

Alex knew someone else's success should not make him feel jealous or slighted. Like Alex, Rob had been with the company for over fifteen years and had worked hard on several major projects with Rob in a business development role and Alex on the software engineering and innovation side of things. But he couldn't help feeling negative toward the news.

When would Alex's turn come to see such an announcement detailing his incredible contributions to the company, congratulating him on being rewarded with a VP position?

That the board was thinking of bringing in someone external to fill the VP of Innovation role was bad enough. But to promote Rob to Associate VP of Business Development? Rob Langley? Sure, he worked hard and was good at his job. But that smug attitude. He imagined the grin Rob must have had on his face with his new promotion. How long until he would stop by Alex's office to rub it in? Was that the type of behavior that would get you rewarded at DelTech? Is that the type of company Alex still wanted to work for?

What first attracted him to the company were the values they promoted and genuinely lived each day—family, humility, integrity. Yet, over the past five years, as the company continued to grow, Alex had noticed the culture transitioning away from those values and inching closer and closer towards a place that encouraged and rewarded selfish, and greedy behavior. Perhaps not by design, but an unintended consequence of the high-growth, high-pressure environment they had created.

Alex and Rob had started at DelTech around the same time, back when the company was much smaller. Brought in as young, ambitious, and moldable proteges, they actually hit it off as friends in the beginning. Both worked hard, brought great ideas to the table, and were driven by the idea of individual success. But over the years, something about Rob began to rub Alex the wrong way. His ambition and drive started to look more like arrogance and pride. Is that what Alex looked like to others? He hoped not. He could not stand the thought of others seeing him the same way he now viewed Rob Langley.

Alex looked at the fresh cup of tea in his hand, which was poured into a company mug with the DelTech logo splashed across the front and back. He squeezed the mug tighter than usual, like he was giving it a death grip. Picking up his nighttime anxiety pill, he washed it down with a sip of tea. Was it just his imagination, or was the pill a tougher one to swallow tonight?

He could no longer think about the multitude of unread emails and decided to shut down for the day.

It was during his talk with Carolina in bed that night where he hatched his plan. Things were going to change for Alex, for Carolina, for Martin, and for DelTech.

Tomorrow, he would deliver his news to Stacy.

CHAPTER REFLECTION QUESTIONS

✔ Does the idea of taking a vacation from work cause you stress as you think about how much work will pile up while you are away?

- ✔ Do you have time in your calendar each day, each week, to allow yourself time to think and relax your brain?

- ✔ Have you ever gotten to the point where you know you need to make drastic changes in your work life in order to improve your home life?

Chapter 3

Stacy and Alex faced each other ten feet apart. They had met here in her office many times in the past, but not like this. Alex was looking at the person that had been mentoring him, pushing him, and promoting him up through the company. Stacy was looking at her protégé, knowing something was off.

"What was so urgent that you wanted to meet one-on-one today?" Stacy asked with a look of skeptical curiosity. "We have our regular meeting scheduled for Thursday. Anything urgent with the SlickPay project I need to know about?"

Alex looked back at her, almost frozen. He had wondered if she would assume his request to meet would be to deliver bad news. He also assumed she'd figure it was related to the SlickPay project. But that project was in great shape. There were the typical challenges and unforeseen obstacles that come with every software project, but Alex was on top of them.

Yes, Stacy would likely see the information he was about to share with her as bad news, but it was not project related. Emotions ricocheted through him as he anxiously went over his prepared speech in his head. As skilled as he was at artfully delivering unpleasant news to Stacy about an unexpected wrinkle in a project, Alex felt considerably unprepared for the type of conversation he was about to have with his no-nonsense, tough-minded boss.

All morning, Alex dealt with a gnawing ache in the pit of his stomach. It was there when he woke up, clinging tightly as he tried and failed to eat his breakfast and not letting go during the ride into work.

Alex was so deep in thought on the car ride, he couldn't even remember traveling the streets when he pulled into his parking space. The ache in his stomach had been a passenger with him all morning leading up to this conversation with Stacy.

His knees had felt weak on the walk into Stacy's office, and he almost tripped as he entered. It was a feeling he couldn't remember having since his wedding day sixteen years earlier, a few short months before he started working at DelTech.

"No, this isn't about SlickPay," Alex responded. "In fact, it isn't about any of the projects on my plate. This is about me." Stacy had been vulnerable with Alex eight years ago when she opened up to him about her divorce. This created some trust. Alex felt like he could be open with her now in return.

Stacy eased back into the cushy office chair behind her massive mahogany desk. The look on her face was almost as if she had been waiting for this conversation and it had finally arrived. Despite their relationship, this was going to be a difficult conversation. The ache inside Alex grew more prominent. Like a hot iron was being poked into his belly and then twisted for good measure.

"Listen, Alex, I've been working hard to get you the VP role. If you're upset because the board hasn't agreed yet, I get it." Stacy was about to go on when Alex mustered up the courage to interrupt.

"This isn't about the VP position or the board," Alex explained. "It's about me and where I am at in my life right now."

"What do you mean?" Stacy seemed confused.

"I'm forty-one years old with a high profile, high paying job at a successful company. I have a nice big house, a great car, a loving wife, and a terrific son I adore."

"Yes, you have it pretty good," Stacy said, smiling and nodding her head as she reflected on Alex's list of life accomplishments. "A lot of people would envy what you have."

"And yet, despite all these things, I feel like I'm squandering my life. Is money really a good barometer of happiness?"

Alex sat down in one of the guest chairs in Stacy's office and pulled it closer to her desk. He needed to give context about what he was trying to explain. Now that the conversation had started, the ache was starting to subside. Somewhat. He needed to press on and get it out.

"I am sure on the outside looking in, it would appear like I have it all. But the truth is, I barely spend any quality time with Carolina or Martin anymore. It's like we live in the same house and are living completely different lives. Martin is starting to turn into quite the hockey player, and I have only seen him play three times all season. And the season is almost over. Carolina is a super mom that takes care of the house, does the grocery shopping, cooks all the meals, and is practically raising Martin on her own while I put in sixty to seventy hours a week here at DelTech. And for what?" The ache was getting smaller with each word he spoke.

"I had no idea you felt like this, Alex." Stacy was clearly taken aback by his admission. "I thought you thrived off your work here at DelTech. You have always been such a high achiever, and I have been trying for years to keep giving you more challenges. I thought it was important that you had work that you found both challenging and rewarding. And you never failed to deliver." Stacy was building her case.

This was her defense for the part she had played in Alex getting to where he was at. And what point was he exactly at? A breaking point? Was he about to resign?

"Yes, I know," Alex answered her. "I am a high achiever and a workaholic. If left to my own devices, I may even work upwards of eighty hours a week just to do the best job I can. But here I am, forty-one years old and taking anxiety medication to try to deal with the situation I've created for myself. And I mean that. Stacy, I don't blame you. This is my own fault. I have tied my happiness to these milestones that I keep pushing further down the field. I fool myself into thinking the next raise, the next promotion, the nicer car is going to bring me happiness. But I see now that they won't. It has become an endless treadmill with no destination."

"So, what are you telling me here, Alex. Be candid with me."

"I need to change the path I'm on."

This conversation he was having with Stacy felt surreal. Almost like a couple breaking up. It's not you it's me.

"Meaning what?"

"Meaning I no longer have the goal of being a VP here at DelTech. In fact, I no longer have the goal to remain as Senior Director of Innovation. I need to change the priorities in my life." Alex exhaled. He finally released the words he had been rehearsing in his head all morning.

"So, you're resigning?" Stacy was looking for clarification.

"Not exactly, at least not right now."

"What are you telling me then?" Stacy looked confused and impatient with the seeming vagueness of the conversation.

"I would like to help you find someone to replace me in my senior director position. Once that person is in place and up to speed, I will move into a part-time advisory role." The pitch had been made. Alex let it sit in an uncomfortable silence. He watched Stacy's face for a reaction. But she was tough to read.

Later that evening, Alex replayed the entire conversation for Carolina, who was desperate to hear the details. She knew how nervous he had been to have the meeting with Stacy and present his plan.

"Wow, that took a lot of courage for you, Alex. I am proud of you for wanting to take this leap of faith," Carolina said as she gave Alex a hug.

"I wasn't sure how it was going to go. Would she be open to the idea? Or would she fire me on the spot?" Alex used his hands to represent scales as he weighed the two different paths Stacy could have taken.

"Well, I am glad to hear she was receptive," Carolina responded.

"Eventually. She didn't seem too enthused about the idea, initially. But as we continued to talk about it, she saw I was serious, and I think she realized it was in her best interest to keep me around. We agreed to have me stay on full-time in my role for six months while we find a replacement and get them up to speed." Alex laid out the specifics of the plan he and Stacy had come up with.

"And then what?"

"There the plan turns a little fuzzy. I proposed staying on part-time for a while. Stacy is not sure the board will agree to that arrangement. She's not even sure what sort of role would be available for me in that capacity. So, we'll continue to discuss that over the next six months. She did say she'll go to bat for me with the board."

Carolina rolled her eyes. "You've heard that promise before."

"I know. But I feel good knowing I have at least six months to think more about my future. Our future. And determine how to live the life I want to live. Not the life DelTech wants me to live." Alex felt like a huge weight had been lifted from his shoulders. He felt lighter. The ache in his stomach was completely gone. He could now create a new life where he and Carolina could spend much more quality time together, and he could watch Martin play hockey, even help coach his team next season. Life was going to be great.

The clock was now ticking, though. He had six months to determine and implement a plan for the next chapter of his life. Little did he realize that the ache would come back as a passenger in Alex's belly many more times in the future for different reasons. But, for now, Alex felt great.

Over the next few weeks, Alex found himself leaving work at a reasonable hour most days and enjoying dinner and relaxing evenings at home with Carolina and Martin. To his surprise, work at DelTech continued as normal. Projects did not fall into a crisis because Alex was not working until ten or eleven each night. Other people on his teams picked up the slack and seemed to relish their new opportunities as Alex began to take a step back.

Had he been holding some people back, Alex wondered? Was he actually helping the company in the past with all those late nights and weekends spent glued to his computer? Or had he injected himself as a bottleneck, denying other people the chance to shine? Alex was sure he knew the answer.

This would be the first time—of many—that Alex would question his decision to leave DelTech. Should he have just made some smaller changes and delegated more work to others? Would that have been enough to give him the life he wanted? More time with Carolina and Martin? Less stress? Alex had some doubts about the path he was now on. But he had made his decision and set a plan in motion with Stacy. He needed to see it through.

With the newfound extra time, he was able to think about what he wanted to do with his career since the day would come when he'd no longer be a DelTech employee.

Would it make sense for him to move to a different company and start fresh? Or would he merely end up in the exact same place, working long hours as a high-achieving workaholic chasing down the next promotion?

Could he start his own software company? He had a lot of ideas and a large network of highly-skilled people he could hire. The fantasy of being the founder of the next big tech startup excited him. But it also seemed like a daunting task, one that would also lead him towards the life he was hoping to escape.

There were times when Alex even dreamed of having a job with no high-pressure responsibilities.

Maybe work at the local hardware store. Perhaps he could be a mailman, walking the streets, delivering letters and bills and flyers to people. Something with minimal stress where he could keep busy, but not have the weight of the world on his shoulders. The pressure he had been under at DelTech the past several years had been crippling. His doctor still had him taking his anxiety medication. Some days, this idea of taking a menial job seemed to be the most appealing option.

For now, Alex concentrated on helping Stacy find the best candidate to replace him. The position had been posted and there was no shortage of suitors for the job.

On one hand, Alex was eager to find and help transition all the responsibilities over to the new eager recruit, molding them to lead his teams and projects. On the other hand, Alex wondered if he should warn the next person not to get too attracted to the allures of the job: the money, the title, the prestige.

Should he give them a glimpse of what it could do to their personal life? Should he warn them that they could be jeopardizing their health, their marriage, and any interests outside of work?

Or was that just Alex? Was he wired in such a way that he would have wound up in this situation regardless of the position or the company? Alex still had some soul searching to do if he wanted to answer this question.

As the weeks passed, a new replacement for Alex's role was eventually selected. Geraldine Briggs came with an impressive resume, having led product development teams at a few major software companies over the past dozen years. Armed with an MBA, she came full of creative new ideas for the SlickPay product and many others in the DelTech portfolio. She did not take long to dig in and get up to speed. Alex would continue to train and mentor her for the next two months, making sure she was set up for success.

Alex was equal parts relieved and concerned. A sharp new mind was there to take over his teams and his projects. The relief came from the feeling of being able to take the foot off the gas and slow down. He would soon be able to finally have a real vacation with his family again.

But he also felt jealousy. Alex watched Geraldine acclimate herself to DelTech. His peers were now her peers, too. No longer Stacy's protégé, a post now filled by his own replacement, he was a mere observer to the transition.

It was also starting to set in that he was not as indispensable as he liked to think. A big part of Alex had always felt that DelTech would not be able to operate without him. He was too important. Watching his new replacement fit seamlessly into his role told him otherwise.

"Geraldine," Stacy called out. "Can you come to my office? I want to run some ideas past you and get your opinion." It was a request Alex had heard Stacy make many times, except it was normally his name she was calling. Hearing his name replaced with Geraldine's made him feel empty inside.

Was his opinion no longer valued? Had he given up too early on something he should have kept pursuing? Was he close to becoming VP where he could then redesign his life once he was in the position? With someone from outside the company now in place to take over his role, would she be on a fast track to the VP position, a position he had coveted for so long? A new type of ache was forming in the pit of his stomach.

Alex knew he had to put those thoughts behind him. He had a new chapter in his life to plan.

But that was precisely what was causing Alex apprehension. Someone was now taking over his role. It was really happening, and the clock was now ticking faster and approaching zero. With only two more months to go until his full-time employment was to end, he needed to nail down a plan for his next steps.

"Geraldine, can you come to my office? I want to run some ideas past you and get your opinion." Those words played over and over again in his head. Geraldine was the new Alex. And now who was he?

As Geraldine emerged from Stacy's office, Alex heard his boss's familiar voice as she peeked her head out and locked eyes with him. "Alex, can we speak for a minute?"

Alex felt instantly reassured. Stacy wanted his opinion, too. Perhaps Geraldine had brought her some ideas and Stacy wanted to bounce them off Alex? Maybe she had an update from the board about the plan to keep him on part-time, his skillset and experience valued by DelTech, after all.

"Come on in and close the door." Stacy sat at her desk and waved him forward, indicating for him to take a seat. She looked emotionless. Almost cold.

Alex's excitement and feeling of value and worth to the company soon left his body completely at the sight of her face. The next words out of her mouth drained him of any positive feelings.

"We have decided to make a change," she said, her tone very matter of fact. She was no longer looking directly at Alex. Her eyes wandered to various spots around the office, anywhere but his eyes. Was she avoiding the look on his face? "With Geraldine now in place and up to speed, we feel it is redundant to have you both in your current roles."

"What does this mean? Am I moving into the part-time role earlier than expected?"

"No."

"Then what?" It was Alex's turn to be direct with Stacy.

"The board feels there is no role for you here at DelTech. We are terminating your employment without cause. You will receive a nice severance package." Everything Stacy said from that point on was a blur.

What had he done? This was not supposed to be the plan. He didn't have anything lined up yet. Alex had effectively found his own replacement, trained her to the point where he was expendable, and now here he was ... expendable.

Didn't DelTech value him and all the time and effort he had poured into his work over the years? Was it actually the board that made this decision, or was it Stacy and she had used the board as a scapegoat? Was it the board that had been holding him back from the VP position all this time, or was it Stacy?

An HR rep walked him through the details of his severance package, and then asked him to hand over his company laptop, cell phone, and security badge. His access to company email, network folders, and all software platforms were disabled within minutes. He was then asked to leave the office immediately.

He could come back after-hours to collect his personal items from his office, which would be packaged into boxes and left for him at reception.

The entire experience seemed surreal. So many thoughts and emotions flooded into him over the next few hours. Anger, bitterness, betrayal, hurt, emptiness, confusion. His head was spinning and thumping like a lopsided washing machine on the rinse cycle.

THUMP ... THUMP ... THUMP.

The veins in his temples throbbed as he attempted to clear his thoughts.

Alex didn't drive straight home. Instead, he drove aimlessly around the city for a while as his brain tried to make sense of what had just happened. How would he tell Carolina? What would she say?

While driving around with no fixed destination, Alex faced temptations. He was tempted to call Stacy and give her a piece of his mind. He was tempted to stop at every fast-food chain he passed and feed his sorrows. He was tempted to just keep driving so as not to have to face the reality of the situation.

But, in the end, he knew he had to face it head on. He needed to come up with a plan. He needed to talk it through with Carolina.

"Are you serious? After everything you have done for that company? For Stacy?" Carolina was incredulous, her fiery Chilean side rising to the surface. Alex had been the cause of that fire a few different times in their marriage. As a husband, he had committed his share of unintentional, thickheaded blunders over the years. There was relief in knowing he was not the cause of her fiery passion at the moment.

"I feel so empty right now. What a fool I was to think they would still need or want my services."

"They are the fools, Alex. Not you."

"Thanks, Carolina. But what do I do now? I thought I would have much more time to come up with a plan for my next steps. Now, I feel the pressure to figure it out immediately."

They discussed the situation, reviewing the details of his severance package, and crunched some numbers. After a sober second thought, they both calmed down, realizing they were not in as dire straits as they had first imagined. There was enough there to hold them through while they figured things out.

Carolina suggested she be the one to find a job. She had not been working outside the home since Martin was born. Her staying home to raise Martin was a decision they had carefully made together, not that she begrudged for a second her role as a stay-at-home parent. But she did miss several aspects of the working world. There was something about being around other adults and being part of a team that were working towards a common vision or goal. Carolina formerly practiced as a legal secretary and knew she could easily find work again. Besides, Alex had been working so hard at DelTech the past sixteen years and could use a break.

They tossed around the idea of them both getting jobs, but quickly decided it would not be the best for Martin. Already neglected by one parent for the past few years, they couldn't hope or expect friends and family to handle his busy extracurricular schedule.

Ultimately, they decided to stick with the original plan to have Alex find a career more conducive to a better work-life balance. But what?

It was in church on a particular Sunday when the idea came to him. Pastor Johnson was reminding the congregation about the temptations of conforming to society. This time, Alex was paying closer attention to the pastor's words.

"'Do not conform to the pattern of this world, but be transformed by the renewing of your mind.'" It was a quote from the Apostle Paul in the Book of Romans.

Of course, Paul was referring to turning away from the temptations of the sinful ways of the world and committing your mind to the ways of Jesus. Alex knew this, yet he couldn't help but begin to think about society's expectations for adult life.

Get a post-secondary education.

Get a steady job at a good company, utilizing your post-secondary education.

Get married and buy a house.

Rely on your job to pay down your student debt, pay off your mortgage, and save for retirement.

Hope that you save enough money to enjoy retirement at the age of sixty-five and not be a burden to your kids.

Starting from a young age, this was the script we were told to follow. A proven model. Safe. But it also required the individual to put a lot of their eggs into someone else's basket, like Alex had been doing with DelTech.

"Do not conform to the pattern of this word." Alex replayed the words in his head.

What about the people that wanted to take a different path? What about those who wanted to create and build? Those who wanted to bet on themselves? These people were generally seen as eccentric or rule breakers. But did that mean it was wrong to take a different path?

Pastor Johnson continued to read from Romans. "'We have different gifts, according to the grace given to each of us.'"

Gifts, yes. Alex remembered taking the spiritual gifts survey a few years back when they first joined the church. His gifts were leadership, knowledge, and teaching. These things came naturally to him. They invigorated him. Could he use his gifts in a different way, a way he hadn't considered before?

An idea was starting to form in Alex's mind. He thought back to the recent strategy sessions at DelTech, the ones with the outside consultants. He thought about how great it must be to come in and spend a few days with different companies, helping them brainstorm, strategize, and set the direction of the company. He thought again about how everyone would hang off the consultant's every word, like it was from God himself.

His mind continued to wander. He thought of Rob Langley and the idea he'd brought to the last strategy session. It was ridiculous in Alex's mind. Why wasn't his idea shot down by anyone on the leadership team? They'd all just nodded their heads slowly. Either they were trying to find the right word to politely dismiss his idea, or they were just as insane as Rob to think it was a good one. Huh ... Rob Langley, VP of Business Development. Alex clenched his fists tightly just thinking about Rob's recent promotion.

But enough about Rob. Just imagine if he was the consultant leading those sessions. How great would that be?

A nudge and a look from Carolina, who could tell Alex's mind was wandering, brought him out of his wandering. The look was not of the usual patient and loving variety. He jolted up in his seat and turned his attention back to Pastor Johnson's message—for a few minutes anyway. At the very least, he was absorbing the theme of this week's sermon. But now, his mind was racing with excitement over his new idea.

Alex wondered what it would be like to be on the other side of the table. To be the consultant. To be seen as the expert with great ideas. It wasn't a fully formed plan yet, but Alex left church that Sunday with the intent of starting his own consulting practice, along with some guilt for missing the true meaning of the message that Sunday. As per usual, in his mind, he was taking what Pastor Johnson was teaching and applying it in a completely different context.

The original plan was to start something as a side hustle while working part-time at DelTech. That would have given him the ability to set out some ideas while minimizing the pressure to immediately generate sustainable revenue. But that plan was no longer an option. Yes, working for sixteen years at DelTech guaranteed a hefty severance package that would sustain him nicely for a while. But the pressure Alex was putting on himself was quite high despite this. He needed to start putting some pieces of a plan in place.

"What should I call my consulting company?" he asked Carolina and Martin later that week during dinner. "Should I just name it after myself: Alex Green Consulting. Or should I give it more of a company name, like The Focus Group?"

"Do you plan on being a solo consultant forever?" Carolina asked. "Or do you have aspirations to grow it into a larger business with other consultants and staff members? If you plan to grow it, naming it after yourself may not be a good idea." How did she always know the right questions to ask?

Martin watched curiously as his parents debated the two different paths Alex could take with his business. After some back and forth, Martin chimed in. "Which option would mean you would be able to come watch my hockey games?" he asked.

Alex and Carolina both stopped talking and eating, seemingly frozen at Martin's question. Alex's eyes met Carolina's, and he knew they both understood what Martin was feeling. In that moment, Alex decided he would be a solo consultant, which would give him more control over his time with his family while also reducing the likelihood he would revert back to his workaholic ways.

He decided, however, he would still go with a more corporate sounding name for his company. Something just didn't sit right with him about naming the company after himself. It come across as prideful or egocentric. Better to go with a more generic name. He was starting to become fond of the name Align. He even had thoughts of what a logo could look like.

Over the next few days, Alex spent time designing his logo, using the latest graphic design software, and setting up a website for his new company. He could already envision potential clients finding his company website online and lining up to work with him. He would announce himself to the world as a business consultant and then things would quickly take off.

His offered services would range from strategic planning to leadership coaching, project management, facilitating innovation brainstorming workshops, and more. The last several years at DelTech provided him with a wide variety of experience and expertise. Combine that with his gifts of teaching, and companies would be banging down his door to work with him.

Only, it didn't work out that way. At all.

His website for Align had been up for three weeks and few people had visited it according to Google Analytics. The few that did land on his website were likely family and friends whom he had sent the link to directly.

Unfortunately, one of the people that visited his site was Rob Langley, who was now firmly entrenched in his VP role at DelTech. Alex knew he'd visited the site because he ran into Rob at the grocery store one evening in the frozen food section.

"Saw your website. Good luck with your little venture." The words alone could be interpreted as a genuine expression of well wishes. But this was coming from Rob Langley, who said it with a smug smirk and a condensing look on his face.

Little venture? Those words stung. It was as if Rob was already foreseeing that Alex's consulting company wouldn't amount to much. It was a shot at Alex for not pursuing the VP position that was perpetually dangled in front of him at DelTech. But Alex just smiled back at Rob as if he was taking what he said as an actual compliment. Alex placed a frozen lasagna in his cart and kept walking. Letting Rob get under his skin wouldn't help him at the moment. He needed to figure out how he was going to land his first consulting engagement.

Especially with nobody visiting his site. No prospective clients had filled out the contact form on his website. His phone had not even ringed.

He gave himself two more months to start bringing in some revenue through Align. Any longer without income and he would be relying too much on his savings and severance package. Could he do it? Or should he start checking the job sites for another role he could jump right into, ensuring that he wouldn't put his family in a difficult position? That would allow him to pocket his severance money. He could invest it in stocks or maybe use it as a down payment on a rental property. That money could be put to great use, rather than squandering it away as he tried to start a new business from scratch.

The new stress of starting his own business was slowly replacing the stress he'd walked away from at DelTech. Good thing he was still taking his anxiety meds. For now, Alex was determined to continue betting on himself. But he still had the question of how he would he get his first paying client?

His time at DelTech had prepared him well to work with all kinds of businesses. He was nicely equipped to understand their challenges and help them design and implement new strategies. But his time at DelTech did not prepare him at all when it came to understanding how to market and sell his services. This was new territory, he would soon discover, that would be a major element of his new life.

His first lesson in marketing was not quite what he was expecting.

"I've had a look at your site, and I have some observations as well as some questions for you, Alex." Mikaela Brooks was the Marketing Manager at DelTech and someone Alex respected greatly. She had implemented a new marketing strategy for the company about six years ago that saw them completely change how they communicated with their customers. She was currently working on the marketing strategy for the SlickPay launch. Once Alex realized he had no idea how to properly market his new venture, Align, he went to Mikaela for advice.

Since he was no longer employed with the company, they had agreed to meet for lunch at a restaurant down the street from the DelTech office. This would allow Mikaela to meet with Alex, give him advice, and get back to work. The healthy food options at the place were perfect as Alex was starting to eat better and hadn't had an emergency pizza or double cheeseburger in several weeks. Lunch with Mikaela was on him, in appreciation for her time and expertise.

"I'm listening," Alex responded. He was eager to get some help, but was certain Mikaela would be impressed with his website and could provide suggestions for tweaks he could make.

"First a quick observation about your website, and then the follow up questions." The look on Mikaela's face indicated to Alex she was a bit hesitant to give her feedback. "My observation is that your website advertises you as a generalist when what you want is to be seen as an expert."

This seemed like more than just a minor tweak. She was basically saying that the entire theme of his site was wrong. "I list my background, my experience, and my certifications," Alex answered defensively. He was proud of the work he had put into the website and how nice it looked.

"Yes, you do. And that is great for establishing some credibility," Mikaela explained. "But to be seen as an expert, you need to clearly identify the specific challenge you can solve and for whom," she elaborated. "When done well, the right people landing on your site will feel like you are speaking to them. Right now, your site is not speaking to anyone in particular. You are trying to speak to any and all businesses saying you can help them with an assortment of challenges. You are marketing yourself as a generalist. When you do this, you end up appealing to nobody. Or at least, not the types of clients you actually want to attract."

"So, I should narrow it down to a specific challenge that I help solve," Alex repeated the advice back to her.

"That's correct."

"But won't I lose out on a bunch of work I could be doing?" Alex seemed skeptical of the "expert" strategy Mikaela was suggesting.

"It seems counterintuitive, I know, but trust me. Marketing is all about being crystal clear on whom you are speaking to," Mikaela responded. "Which leads to other questions you should be contemplating."

"Hit me. Ask away." Alex was well aware that marketing was not his strength. He needed all the advice he could get.

"Write these down and take time to think about them. Let's reconnect soon to discuss your answers. First, narrow down your services to the one specific one where you want to be seen as the expert."

"How would I go about narrowing this list down?"

"Great question. I am not a guru when it comes to marketing consulting services, but my advice would be to list each of your current services and determine which ones you are best equipped to solve, which ones you think there is the most demand for, and which ones you would most enjoy solving. Add in any other factors you think differentiates these services. Score them in these areas and see if a clear winner emerges."

"Sounds like a good exercise." Alex was warming up to the idea. "What's the next question I should think about?"

"Once you have identified the specific challenge you will help solve as the 'expert,' you should do a similar problem to determine a specific type of client that you will help. It could be businesses in a specific industry, a specific size of business, or one that's at a certain phase in their growth. Again, the idea is to narrow it down enough so that when someone from one of these businesses lands on your website, they feel like you are speaking to them."

"Makes sense." Alex was already attempting to answer Mikaela's questions.

"Then, finally, think about why these businesses should choose you, and not a different consultant, to help them solve their problem."

"Which is where my skills and experience come in. My track record at DelTech should be pretty convincing." Alex was happy that something on his website was providing value.

"Yes, that's one point in your favor. But there are a few other factors that will help convince people you are the right choice."

THE PARABLE —————— Chapter 3

SOLOPRENEUR LESSON—YOUR NICHE

When starting any new business, be clear on the following:

- ❯ Who is my ideal client? (Be as specific as possible.)
- ❯ What is the specific challenge I will help them solve?
- ❯ How will they benefit from my product/service?
- ❯ Why will they choose me, my product, or my service rather than the competition?

"Such as?"

"Customer testimonials."

"But I haven't had any customers yet," Alex said. It seemed like a chicken and egg scenario. He needed testimonials to attract clients. But he needed clients in order to get testimonials.

"So think of some ways you can get some. Perhaps when you identify the specific challenge you want to be known for solving, you could propose doing a pilot project with a few businesses at a reduced rate, or even free in exchange for some testimonials. I have some other ideas on how to earn some, but don't worry about this point too much at the moment," Mikaela said, trying to ease Alex's mind. "Testimonials will eventually come as you work with more and more businesses. We just need to get the ball rolling."

SOLOPRENEUR LESSON— TESTIMONIALS

Customer testimonials act as great social proof, building trust for new potential clients.

❯ Make sure your testimonials describe the challenges the customer was facing, the benefits they received, and why they chose you.

❯ Collect testimonials in the beginning by doing work for free or at a heavily discounted rate.

"So what other factors will help convince people I am the right choice?"

"Demonstrate that you have the proven solution, one that clearly and effectively addresses their challenge. Remember, people are not looking to purchase your time or your expertise. They are looking to purchase a solution to their problem. So that is what you need to market."

"Give me an example."

"Instead of selling clients your time at a certain rate per hour, sell them a solution at a set price. For example, you could sell an exclusive three-step approach to strategic planning where the client pays $10,000."

"In that case, they see the product as the three-step approach they're buying, rather than just me, my expertise, and my time."

"Exactly."

"So much to think about." Alex was suddenly feeling overwhelmed. He had six weeks before his self-imposed deadline would be reached. Six weeks to determine his services, his ideal customer, his solution, how to properly market Align, and how to gain some paying clients.

He left his lunch meeting with Mikaela more doubtful about his new venture. Part of him felt another pang of regret for proposing his plan to Stacy. Why would he plan to find his own replacement and put himself in a position to be let go? But what was done was done. Six weeks to go.

Time to roll up the sleeves and get to work.

CHAPTER REFLECTION QUESTIONS

✔ Are you following a certain script for your life based on the expectations of others?

✔ Before deciding to start your own solopreneur journey, ask yourself what potential mentors you have in your network you can learn from and rely on for guidance.

✔ What specific gifts do you have to help solve a specific challenge for a specific group of people?

Chapter 4

At the age of seventeen, at the height of his hockey domination, Alex scored four goals in the championship game. All the hard work, all the practice, all the determination culminated in his performance in that final game. Alex could not be stopped that day, willing his team to victory.

His fourth and final goal came in overtime, sealing a thrilling come from behind five to four victory against his team's arch rival, The Rangers. It was a back-and-forth series with Alex and his teammates taking the best-of-seven series four games to three on the back of Alex's incredible final game feat. The memories he had from that game were still etched in his mind. The sight of his teammates jumping on the ice to celebrate the win, the sound of the fans cheering his name, the look of joy and pride on his parents' faces as they watched their son's hard work pay off. The elation he felt that day had only been equalled on two other occasions: his wedding day and the day Martin was born.

"The Game," as Alex and his old hockey friends still refer to it, was a shining moment in Alex's life. It was a moment that felt like a lifetime ago, but also a moment that felt like it just happened yesterday. The memories would stick with him forever.

Alex always seemed to have the internal drive to excel and push himself. His parents would even have to ask him to cut back on all the extra time he would spend practicing his skating and shooting. He would spend hours in the backyard rink during the winter and on the driveway in the warmer months, taking shots over and over into the net. His mother and father both supported him and loved his determination, but also worried about his inability to pull back, to relax, and to deal with not being the best. Had they seen something in Alex that he needed to protect himself against?

But in that fateful championship game at the age of seventeen, all his hard work and the will to succeed had paid off. His team won the championship and Alex was the hero.

The adrenaline rush he felt today was what brought back those memories. They say there are not many feelings that compare to when an entrepreneur makes their first sale. This was what Alex was experiencing at the moment. Not quite the same as "The Game," his wedding, or the birth of his son, but he knew this too would be etched into his memory forever.

"WorkRight accepted my proposal!" he screamed as he got up from the chair in his home office and quickly ran into the kitchen to bring the news to Carolina. This is something he had been driving towards for several weeks now on a rather bumpy road.

Just a few days ago, Alex had been seriously considering pulling the plug on the Align experiment. After initially taking the advice he received from Mikaela about how to market himself as an expert on a niche need, he had found a second wind. However, that burst of enthusiasm hadn't lasted long after he'd completely changed his website and still was not receiving any inquiries. Hockey had seemed to come much easier to Alex. Sure, he had to put in the work, but he had so much natural talent. Building a consulting business from scratch was a completely different challenge altogether, one that did not come naturally to Alex.

One thing Alex had discovered was that he needed to learn how to network and get his name out there. His original strategy of building a website and hoping the right people would find him and reach out was terribly flawed. Mikaela's advice about the copy on the website was spot on, but Alex also needed to first build a trusted network. The website might help close a sale, but it likely wasn't going to open new doors on its own. For that, Alex needed to build some relationships and earn some trust.

Alex went out and joined a few business networking groups and became a member of the local Chamber of Commerce, attending every event he could. He soon found himself making many new connections and perfecting his elevator speech.

"I help medium-sized companies find new innovative ways to deliver value to their customers and double their revenue." It was a sentence he had practiced and perfected many times. It was the answer he now gave every time someone he met at a networking event asked the inevitable question: "So, what do you do?"

He chose medium-sized companies as his sweet spot because what he did was help companies better understand their customers and then find new innovative ways to serve them. By nature, small start-up companies either already were doing well or didn't have the budget for consultants. Larger organizations already had people, or even teams, in charge of these types of things. It was the medium-sized businesses that needed help in this area and could likely afford to bring in some external expertise.

Of course, Alex had a lot more to say about what he did and how, but this was the opening statement that would prompt people to ask the follow-up questions that would allow him to elaborate.

He was now one week away from his self-imposed deadline to land a paying client or put his efforts towards finding a new full-time job. He knew he and Carolina were fine financially and could sustain several months of no income while Alex ramped up his consulting business, but he didn't like that idea. He hated the idea of them using up too much of his severance or their savings in order to prop up his new venture.

So when he received the email from Mark Brown at WorkRight informing him the engagement proposal had been approved, Alex was on cloud nine.

"That's terrific." Carolina smiled warmly at Alex's news. "This is the company you met at that networking even last month?"

"Yeah, they have a project management platform they sell to enterprise organizations. It's called WorkRight. It helps companies plan and track their work. They have plateaued the past few years and are looking to have me help them brainstorm some new ideas. I outlined a three-phased engagement for them, and we've agreed to proceed with the first two phases for now. We'll discuss executing the third phase in the future."

Caroline always took a genuine interest in Alex's work. She asked questions and then follow-up questions, wanting to know the ins and outs of his process. Was he as attentive when it came to asking her about her days as a super mom and wife? Alex knew he was blessed to have such an amazing wife and needed to do better in this department as a husband.

"In the first phase," Alex answered one of her questions, "I will be facilitating some customer feedback research and then analyzing the insights we receive. In phase two, I will be conducting brainstorming sessions with different groups within WorkRight to come up with new innovative ideas based on the customer insights." The idea of packaging his services into a three-step solution had come from his discussions with Mikaela. He had developed processes and templates for each phase and piloted them with small free engagements in exchange for customer testimonials. He was now in a great position to outline his services and give the testimonials inside his proposal document, thereby increasing his credibility.

"You will do a great job, I know it." Carolina was very supportive. "What is phase three and why is that not yet included?" Another great follow-up question.

"The third and final phase will be to pick the top ideas from the brainstorming sessions and determine how we can pilot them to some customers. Since we don't yet know the ideas, we agreed that phase three could be scoped out once phase two is completed. They may or may not need my help implementing the pilot projects. We'll decide that when the time comes. For now, I have lots to dig into with them."

Alex could not wipe the smile off his face if he tried. Over the past few months, he had been on a roller coaster ride of emotions. The highs came whenever he learned something new. Building his website, learning how to package and market his services, mastering the networking scene, were all skills that were brand new to Alex, and he loved to learn and grow. On the other hand, the pressure to find his first client, the pressure to make some income through his new consulting practice—pressure he was putting on himself—was immense.

There were several moments where he had thought about giving up and just finding another job. Checking the job listings in the area at one point became a daily habit. He almost applied to two different jobs that interested him. But Carolina had reminded him each time that if he quit now, he would always have regrets. He needed to give it a real shot. She encouraged him to give Align a full year.

At the end of twelve months, they could reassess the situation. If things were going well, he should continue to focus on Align and grow it. If after a year things were not working out, Alex could always find another full-time job and would not have regrets. Leave no "what if" questions on the table. He would have given it his best shot. Having this support and encouragement from Carolina was key.

With the elation of signing his first client, Alex's self confidence was now sky-high. He had dreams of filling his pipeline with more and more engagements like this one with WorkRight. Companies would be lining up to hire Alex Green from Align to come in and get them out of their rut. Surely, there were hundreds of businesses in a similar position to WorkRight within an hour's drive that would be knocking on Alex's door now that he had this consulting thing all figured out.

Alex would soon learn, however, that the roller coaster ride was far from over. There were many more unforeseen challenges awaiting him. But, for now, his adrenaline was running like high-powered fuel through his veins. He had the puck on his stick and the nothing could stop him.

"Are we still going for a walk together after lunch?" Carolina asked. Over the past few weeks, they had made this a new daily ritual. Each afternoon, they would walk together for forty-five minutes, exploring different walking trails, sharing their thoughts, holding hands, stopping to admire various picturesque views of nature, and enjoying each other's company.

Alex had barely driven his Tesla in the past three weeks. A year ago, Alex would open the door to the garage just to admire the car. "Isn't she beautiful?" he would ask himself each time he stole a glimpse of his pride and join. Now, he almost preferred to walk. Simple was better. The Tesla lay abandoned in the garage, only to be used to run the odd errand. Carolina's mini-SUV was much more functional for taking Martin to and from his various sporting events.

The walks were lovely quality time together as husband and wife. But there was one issue. Alex viewed the walks as a way to get exercise. On his Fitbit, he would track his steps, heartrate, and calories burned, each walk a competition against the last one.

For Carolina, the walks were a leisurely way to explore the outdoors and God's creation, to hear the different sounds of the birds, and to see and smell the various flowers in bloom, frequently stopping to explore whatever intrigued her senses.

"Do we really need to stop and look at those flowers? They look just like the last ones we stopped to look at?" Alex, who just wanted to beat his most recent score, would often say.

"Slow down and enjoy the beauty around you," she would answer.

"We can go for a walk," Alex replied, face not moving off his computer screen now. "I just need to dive in and start preparing a bunch of stuff for this engagement with WorkRight."

Carolina's suspicions about whether that day's walk would happen were confirmed later that afternoon when Alex insisted he could not take a break. But tomorrow they would definitely walk again, he assured her. Alex never even noticed her leave as she went for a walk on her own, him still staring intently at his computer.

As Alex consulted for WorkRight over the next few weeks, his afternoon walks with Carolina were mostly put on hold. Rather than five or six walks together a week, they were down to one or two. Carolina would continue walking by herself on the days Alex was "too busy." Did he notice a sense of frustration building in her?

Once this engagement was over, Alex knew they would resume their usual walking schedule. For now, he had work to do.

The first two phases of the engagement had gone better than he could have hoped, and he was proud of his work. Alex had met with eight of WorkRight's top customers and collected valuable insights and feedback about their experience. He asked each one a similar set of questions:

- ✔ What challenges made them seek out a solution to their project and portfolio management needs?

- ✔ How did they go about looking for solutions?

- ✔ What made them decide to go with WorkRight?

- ✔ What was their experience implementing and utilizing their platform?

- ✔ What about WorkRight was giving them the most value?

- ✔ How has their business improved now that they used WorkRight?

- ✔ What challenges were they still facing?

SOLOPRENEUR LESSON—CUSTOMER RESEARCH

All businesses can benefit from collecting feedback and insights from their customers.

- ❯ Get in the habit of doing this on a regular basis.
- ❯ Markets change. People change. Needs change.
- ❯ Never assume you know your customers' challenges and why they decide to buy a product or service.

His goal was to understand the psychology of each customer, their challenges, and their motivations. The insights he was able to gather were a perfect starting point for the brainstorming sessions he then conducted with WorkRight employees.

Alex was thrilled to have such a diverse group of people in the room for his brainstorming sessions he masterfully facilitated. With the customer insights as their jumping off point, he was able to get people from different parts of the company, with various levels of experience, seniority, and backgrounds to share their varied perspectives. They collected some terrific ideas for new creative ways to serve their customers and attract new clients by solving their common challenges.

In total, he conducted four different brainstorming sessions, and then worked with the WorkRight leadership team to review and pick the top five ideas they felt the strongest about piloting and testing.

Phase one and two were a great success by all measures.

"They loved the different ideas that came out of the sessions," Alex beamed as he shared this update with Carolina. "I am meeting with them tomorrow afternoon to discuss the next steps to pilot and test some of these ideas. I'm pretty sure they'll be asking me to facilitate these pilot projects."

"I thought you were going to pick up Martin from school tomorrow afternoon?"

"Was that tomorrow? I have already committed to meeting with WorkRight tomorrow." Alex felt a pang of guilt. He knew Martin looked forward to his time alone with his father.

Alex noticed Carolina take a deep breath as she sighed. "Don't worry about it. I will see if Jackie can pick him up." Carolina and Mateo's mom, Jackie, often took turns dropping off and picking up the two boys from school when needed. It wouldn't be an issue. Was Alex starting a new trend of promising to spend time with Martin only to have work get in the way? Was he slipping back into old habits? It sure seemed like things were headed in that direction.

It turns out WorkRight was pleased with Alex's work and indeed asked him to lead the pilot projects. At first, Alex was excited to have satisfied his first consulting client and have them pay for more of his services. He had especially enjoyed the customer research and brainstorming that he was able to do with a business other than DelTech. It suited his strengths and his gifts. But what he was about to sign up for in phase three was a different ballgame altogether.

His job would be to act as the project manager for these pilot projects. He was given team members to manage and was to attend the WorkRight weekly project status meetings to give updates on their progress. It didn't take long until Alex felt like he was no longer a consultant but a WorkRight employee.

More and more WorkRight meetings were added to his calendar. Emails poured in. Requests for updates and reports with unreasonable deadlines began to come his way. That sinking feeling like he was right back at DelTech soon invaded his senses.

He was no longer seen as the external voice with the fresh new ways of thinking. People no longer hung on his words, excited by the perspectives he brought to the table. He was now just another cog in the wheel. Beyond the urgent emails and status reports, Alex was also dealing with personality conflicts amongst some of his pilot project team members.

Did he do a great job? Of course. That was what Alex did. In fact, he exceeded their expectations with what he was able to deliver and the insights they gained from the pilot projects.

But did he enjoy it? Not in the least.

By a stroke of luck, or maybe fate, just as his work on the pilot projects for Work Right were winding down, Alex received a call from another company asking him to meet and discuss some potential consulting work.

LODEEMA was an upstart pharmaceutical company that was growing quickly. Although they seemed to fit Alex's ideal customer avatar—medium-sized company looking for new innovative ideas to grow their revenue—he had always worked within the software sector. He was intrigued about potentially helping them and loved to learn and take on new challenges. Working with a pharmaceutical company would bring a slew of opportunities for learning and growth.

"Alex, we'd love to extend your time with us and have you help out on some other initiatives as well." Mark Brown from WorkRight was pleased with the results. He had taken a chance to bring Alex in after meeting him at the networking event a few months back. "We have a few projects that are in real trouble, and we think you would do a great job of rescuing them."

With the meeting of his potential new client LODEEMA on the horizon, Alex felt confident in turning down Mark's offer. Although he appreciated Mark and WorkRight for giving him his first real consulting engagement, he had learned enough about what he enjoyed doing and what he didn't. He had learned when to say yes to and when to say no.

What Alex didn't realize was that the type of consulting LODEEMA was looking for was drastically different from the type of work he had done in the first two phases with WorkRight.

"I can't do what they're asking from me," Alex explained to Carolina one day while taking their walk. "I wouldn't know where to start. Plus, it feels like they would need someone with an extensive pharma background." After the introductory call with their VP of Medical Affairs, the excitement Alex was feeling about this potential new engagement was now replaced with fear, doubt, and anxiety.

"How different would this be from what you did with WorkRight?" Carolina asked as she stopped to listen to some birds.

"Completely different. I am not even sure why they reached out to me. And why did we stop walking?" Alex was getting agitated.

"Did you hear that? I think it is a catbird." Carolina was standing completely still, her left ear pointed towards the tree next to them.

"A catbird?"

"Yes, a relative of the mockingbird. They imitate the sounds of other birds or animals. They can make a sound like a cat's meow."

"I don't hear it. It sounds just like any other bird to me." Alex was itching to start walking again and get back to the conversation about LODEEMA.

"Did you turn them down?" Carolina started walking again.

"No, not yet anyway. I told them I would get back to them with my thoughts. I'm a software guy, what do I know about pharmaceuticals. I should have just said yes to WorkRight and kept working with them. At least it was in my wheelhouse."

Alex was starting to feel regret, questioning his decision about not continuing to consult for WorkRight, even though he did not want to take on the type of work they were looking for him to do. He felt regret about leaving DelTech. He had put in so many years and built a great reputation along

THE PARABLE

with a good salary. He had regret about deciding to become a consultant. What did he know about starting his own consulting agency?

"Alex, it's okay." Carolina stopped walking again and touched his arm. Alex looked in her eyes. They were inches apart physically, but in completely different hemispheres emotionally and mentally. "I know that if you decide to take on this work with Loseema, you will do a great job."

"LODEEMA."

"What?"

"It's LODEEMA, not Loseema," Alex abruptly responded, instantly regretting his tone.

"Loseema ... LODEEMA ... whatever." She let his rudeness slide. This time. "I know you, Alex. You will do a great job at whatever you do. Hockey, work, managing the finances. Whatever you put your mind to, you excel at it." Carolina's voice was soft and supportive. She believed in her husband.

"Thanks, hun, but this time I just don't feel confident. After talking to them and getting a better understanding of their needs, for the first time in a long time, I do not feel like I can deliver." Alex was sure this is what imposter syndrome must feel like. Was he an imposter? What made him think he could be an expert consultant?

SOLOPRENEUR LESSON—IMPOSTER SYNDROME

Every solopreneur is going to feel "imposter syndrome" at some point.

❯ Learn which challenges will be good for you to take on and grow your skillsets and which ones are truly over your head and could damage your reputation if you do a poor job.

"Alex, look at me." Carolina pulled his arm a little more, forcing him to face her. She placed her hands on his cheeks and stared him in the eyes. "So say no to this engagement then. Even though I know you would do a fantastic job, I also know you will find another company that needs your help with something you are more comfortable with, and you will do a great job for them too."

"But what if I don't find another company that needs me?"

"Then I know you will succeed at whatever you decide to do next. Just try to enjoy the journey. Find the joy in each day."

Carolina was right. And she always knew what to say to help calm his nerves. Her gentle touch didn't hurt either. The rest of their walk contained much less worry, stress, and talk about Align. Instead, there were blissful moments of holding each other's hand, admiring the beautiful scenery, and even the occasional smooch or two.

Over the next two weeks, Alex felt much better about his situation. He had made enough money through his engagements with WorkRight to hold him over for a while so he could concentrate on refining his services and looking for new clients. He was taking Carolina's advice and embracing the journey.

His days looked different now. At DelTech, Alex was a slave to his calendar. His days were structured so that every possible block of time in his day had to be perfectly planned out. He knew what he was doing each day because it was all in his calendar. He didn't have to think about it.

And now? His days were spent however he decided. This was a tough transition at first. He was used to the routine, the meetings, the structure that came with the corporate world. Now he had to create his own structure and routine. That was an adjustment he wasn't expecting.

SOLOPRENEUR LESSON—THE VALUE OF ROUTINE

- Having routine and structure is a good way to create healthy habits.
- Find ways to carve out focused time for important tasks each day.

Alex chose to spend his mornings reading about sales and marketing and to test out some of the strategies and tactics he was learning. Checking LinkedIn and seeing the types of things people were posting about was another thing he started to do more regularly. Alex did not create videos or write clever and insightful posts, but he enjoyed seeing what others were doing, observing what was capturing and keeping his attention.

But his days again consisted of taking regular walks with Carolina in the afternoon and spending some quality father-son time with Martin when he got home from school. This was a much better pace from what his life was like only a few months ago working at DelTech. No more urgent emails, no pressure-filled deadlines, no promotions or salary increases being dangled in front of him. He was his own boss now.

Alex had even turned down a job offer just last week from a company that reached out to him through a recruiter. In his DelTech days, he may have jumped at this opportunity. Great pay, great company, great position, and a new challenge. But his focus was different now.

He wanted to be the architect of a different life. A life of quality time with Carolina and Martin. A life of balance between work and relaxation. A life of healthy emotional and physical choices. No more anxiety pills. No more fast food. That was Alex's focus now.

After a full month of not having any new consulting work, Alex admitted that he was starting to get a little worried. But he was enjoying the new pace and was finding the joy in each day. The work and the income would eventually come, he told himself.

It was when Alex logged into LinkedIn one day to do his thirty minutes of observing and learning that his world turned upside down.

There it was, sitting in his notifications. Like a cold slap across the face.

"Geraldine Briggs has a new role as VP of Innovation at DelTech. Click here to congratulate her."

Seriously? She had only been there for, what, ten months? Maybe eleven? Alex was floored.

He stared at his laptop screen for a good sixty seconds, an empty stare, trying to process what he just read. He finally clicked on the button that would take him to the post about Geraldine's promotion, the promotion that had been dangled in front of him by Stacy Kincaid for at least three years. The role the board said they wanted to consider giving to an outside person. Well, here she was, Geraldine Briggs, brought in from the outside because Alex decided to step away. He had pretty much handed her this role. Could it have been his if he had stayed? Would he be the VP of Innovation at DelTech now if he was still working there?

Alex knew that clicking on the link to take him to the post would subject him to something he may not want to see: people celebrating the post, people commenting and celebrating on the post that should have been about him.

As his eyes darted through the various comments. He noticed quite a few were from people he did not know. Likely people from Geraldine's former companies. But there were some he did know. Some people from the team he used to lead, the team Geraldine took over.

Congrats, Geraldine. Well deserved!

Way to go, Geraldine.

So happy to have you at DelTech, Geraldine.

Each one stung a little more as Alex read them. His former team. Had they forgotten him? Was Geraldine a better leader than him?

His skin was getting flushed and his chest began to tighten.

Then his eyes came across a comment from Stacy.

What a pleasure it has been having you on the team, Geraldine. Can't wait to see how we will continue to grow with you in this new role!

That one really hurt. Did Alex not help the company grow? He sure did. Year over year. Where was his promotion?

Alex reached for his bottle of anxiety pills. He hadn't taken one in almost three weeks, but he needed one.

Then the dagger.

A comment from Rob Langley.

Geraldine, you are just what DelTech has been missing these past several years. What a breath of fresh air. Welcome to the VP role! I look forward to working more closely with you.

For the next ten minutes, Alex sat slumped in his chair, his hands over his face. A man defeated.

CHAPTER REFLECTION QUESTIONS

- ✔ What networking groups can you join to expand your network and practice your pitch?

- ✔ What opportunities do you have to perform customer research?

- ✔ What type of service do you prefer to provide? Short or long engagements? Workshops? Advisory consulting or hands-on implementation?

- ✔ What do you want your life to look like? How might you design your business around that?

Chapter 5

"It's been eight months since I left DelTech." Alex was doing the math quickly in his head. "Yes, that's right. And I launched Align just a few weeks after I was let go. I guess that means I've officially been a solopreneur consultant for around eight and a half months."

"Let's do a quick recap. In only eight and a half months you have taken a leap of faith by walking away from the corporate job you had been in for over sixteen years." It was Pastor Johnson.

"I was let go," Alex interrupted.

"Yes, but, in effect, you did walk away from that career, right? A job that was consuming your life and robbing you of your health and relationships. You have started a new consulting practice from scratch. You're eating healthier and exercising again."

"I'm down twenty pounds," Alex proudly proclaimed.

"That's great! It seems to me you have a lot to be proud of."

"Yes, but in that same time I have only consulted for three clients. One engagement started out great, but, by the end, I wound up feeling like an employee. With the next two, I ended up lowering my rates, and I felt like they didn't value what I brought to the table. And the real kicker is that I have seen the person who replaced me in my role at DelTech go on to get the promotion I had my sights set on for years." Alex did not feel all that proud about the last eight months. In fact, he felt like a failure and was in need of some encouragement at the moment, which is why he found himself sitting in Pastor Marcus Johnson's office. It was Pastor Johnson's message that past Sunday that prompted Alex to ask him to meet.

Determination and being consistent with your faith was the main theme of the sermon. Two particular verses hit home with Alex that day.

From the book of James: "Blessed is the one who perseveres under trial because, having stood the test, that person will receive the crown of life that the Lord has promised to those who love him."

And from 2 Timothy: "I have fought the good fight, I have finished the race, I have kept the faith."

"You will be faced with trials in life. Face those trials head on with steadfast determination," Pastor Johnson proclaimed to his congregation that day.

Alex, true to form, related the message back to his current situation with Align. He sure was being tested.

He was facing trials. But he wasn't sure if he could face them head on with steadfast determination. That's what prompted him to reach out to Pastor Johnson.

"The thief comes only to steal, kill, and destroy," Pastor Johnson, who was leaning forward now in his office chair, said, referencing a quote from the Book of John. "It seems to me that he has been stealing your joy away from this new journey you are on, while killing and destroying your self confidence." That one hit home. Alex has been a bundle of nerves for a while. "Alex, make no mistake, you have taken a brave step and are achieving some incredible things, even if it's not as quickly as you would like. But try to remember that true happiness is not going to come from your achievements."

Alex was more confused by that last statement. "But I have always subscribed to the mantra that we should set goals for ourselves and then be overjoyed when we achieve them."

"Of course. Be prudent, set goals, and celebrate when you achieve them. But keep in mind that true happiness is not a function of your achievements, but a function of how you spend your time. Your successes will give you a temporary thrill. But your real happiness lies in enjoying the daily activities you do that bring you joy. Learn to find and attach your joy to what you are doing each day."

SOLOPRENEUR LESSON—EMBRACE THE JOURNEY

Starting a business can be very stressful.

- Find ways to enjoy each day.
- Set small goals to achieve and celebrate regularly.
- Reward yourself with pockets of time doing things you enjoy.

"I suppose I may never be happy if I keep looking for my satisfaction in each new goalpost I keep moving farther and farther down the field. I guess I would not have been happy even if I got the VP position at DelTech."

"I suspect not."

"Carolina tells me I need to embrace the joy in the journey," Alex reflected.

"Your wife is a wise lady."

"I keep realizing just how wise she really is."

After a good discussion with Pastor Johnson, and a much better feeling about the current path he was on, Alex was determined to persevere and get past this rough period of self doubt. He had six more months to make Align a viable business before the full year was up. Whether or not he succeeded in making it a stable replacement to his income from DelTech, he was going to soak up the journey.

Another meeting that week also had a large influence on Alex. This one was with Charles Redding, a consultant Alex met at a networking event. He was about five years ahead of Alex and Align with his own consulting practice. He seemed to have things all figured out.

Alex had watched Charles confidently handle himself at a few different networking events. When he spoke to prospective clients, he never sold himself or his services, but always offered valuable expert advice. At first, Alex thought Charles was foolish to be giving away so much advice for free. But he saw how people—past and prospective clients—lined up to talk to Charles at those events. Maybe there was something to giving away free advice? It sure helped make Charles look like an expert and created trust with these people.

Alex was almost shocked when Charles was more than willing to meet him for a coffee and share some guidance about how he started his consulting business. Again, free advice. Again, building trust. Alex was seeing a pattern here.

SOLOPRENEUR LESSON—MENTORS

Pride is the burden of a foolish person.

> ❯ Being a solopreneur does not mean you have to figure everything out on your own.
>
> ❯ Seek out mentors who are a few years ahead of where you are in your journey.

"It seems to me we took two different approaches, in several aspects," Charles explained after listening to Alex describe his journey over the past year.

"How so?" asked Alex, curious to hear about Charles' journey.

"For starters, you made a decision and went all in. I admire your courage."

"How did you get started then?"

"As a side hustle while I was still working full-time. I wanted to first see if it was a viable option before I walked away from my corporate job. On one hand, this allowed me to spend time testing what worked and what didn't without having to rely on my consulting income as my main source of income."

"That was my original plan, as well. It didn't quite work out that way. And on the other hand?"

"On the other hand, it didn't create any sense of urgency. I still had my comfortable job and my comfortable paycheck." Charles shook his head as if he was upset with himself. "It likely took me too long to finally take the leap. But you didn't give yourself a choice. You took the leap and then decided to try to figure things out."

"So which approach is better?" Alex was still in disbelief that Charles Redding had agreed to meet and discuss this with him.

"Let me preface everything else I am about to tell you today with this." Charles looked serious as he was prepared to impart some wisdom. "There is no one set path that we should all take. Sure, there are some proven best practices and some things you should avoid, but we all have our own journey, our own experiences, and our own skillsets. What works for one person may not work for you. So, take whatever you can from my journey only if it makes sense for you."

"Understood. So, how else have our paths been different?"

Charles went on to explain to Alex how he started his consulting purely as a side hustle. First, he started writing regularly on LinkedIn. In his posts, he decided to give away free advice, tips, and examples about managing change, his area of expertise.

Charles observed what types of posts resonated with people and which ones didn't. He observed and repeatedly tweaked his posts until he found his writing voice and a style that worked. The engagement on his posts went up. His connections grew. He built relationships. People eventually began to see Charles as an expert in Change Management. Some people began to reach out to him for advice.

At first, Charles would have video calls with people for free to see what types of challenges they were having and how he could help. Once he knew he had a good solution to the problems he was being asked to help solve, he decided to set up a timeslot each week for paid consulting calls. He would continue to post all kinds of free advice and tips on LinkedIn. But now when people would reach out to Charles for further advice, he would send them a link to book a call with him for $200 an hour.

Only a small percentage of people would book a call, but it proved to Charles that he was providing value that people were willing to pay for.

In those calls, Charles continued to observe and learn. What type of people were paying for the calls? What businesses were they from? What specific challenges were they facing? Why did they decide to have a call with Charles and not someone else? What questions did people continue to ask? How did he need to tweak the advice he was giving?

SOLOPRENEUR LESSON—MORE CUSTOMER RESEARCH

Without customers, you have no business.

> ❯ In order to determine if there is a market for your product or service, test to see if people are willing to pay for it.
>
> ❯ If they are willing to pay for it, then continue to be curious.
>
> ❯ Learn as much as you can about them, their situation, their challenges, and what made them decide to pay for your product or service.

All of this paid learning helped Charles put together a full-blown four-step consulting package aimed at helping a specific type of company solve a specific challenge they were having with employees' resistance to change.

"That's when I finally decided to create a website. Only, I didn't do it myself like you did. I hired a professional. I had my ducks in a row and knew exactly the specific challenge I helped to solve for a specific type of business. They were able to build me a great website very quickly."

"And people started coming to your website? Just like that?"

"No, not at all." Charles was smiling now. "Most people don't just go on the internet and search for a business consultant. They find us through referrals or other channels. But you need a website as a place to send them to learn more about what you do and why they should choose you."

"But you didn't have any customers yet, other than the one-hour calls you did. How did you get people to your site?" Alex was hanging on Charles' every word.

"I leveraged the LinkedIn community I had built. Over the course of a year, while doing this on the side, I had built a pretty good-sized network of around nine thousand people. My posts were getting seen by thousands of people with lots of engagement. So, I wrote a post announcing that I had launched a full-time consulting practice and shared my new website. Word spread quickly. I still have it as a featured post on my LinkedIn profile so anyone new that connects with me will see it."

"Boy, have we taken different paths." Alex slumped in his chair, mentally kicking himself for some of the rash steps he had taken over the past year. Perhaps he should have had a much better plan in place before leaving DelTech. "I started with a website, built by me, thinking that was the holy grail. You, on the other hand, built up a network, built your credibility, and smartly tested out a few approaches before finally launching a website and your offering. I wish I could replay the past year and make different decisions."

"Maybe. Or maybe what I did wouldn't have worked for you at all. Remember, there is no one perfect plan that works for everyone. From what I can see, Alex, you must be doing some things right. I see you at networking events. You have landed some paying

clients. You reach out to people like me for advice."
Charles could see that Alex was being much too
hard on himself. "Those are all great things. Now
you need to determine what next steps to take. Try
things you've learned from my journey. Take what
works for you, drop what doesn't, and keep going."

"Thanks again for agreeing to meet with me, Charles.
I appreciate it."

"I am happy to help. There is more than enough
consulting work to go around. Besides, I had some
great people lending me advice along the way. I try
to pay it forward whenever I can. And by the way,
Alex, it wasn't a simple path for me either. I may
have taken a different route, but I still had many
challenges. Keep at it."

SOLOPRENEUR LESSON—GIVERS

There are plenty of giving people out there.

❯ Don't be afraid to reach out to others for
advice.

❯ Some people may surprise you and be giving
with their time.

❯ Pay it forward and do the same for others.

After his meeting with Charles, Alex was intrigued
by the concept of leveraging LinkedIn. He had been
observing quite a bit over the past few months and

felt like he was ready to start writing some posts. His objective was to learn how to write effectively while growing a network of business leaders that could be potential clients.

At first, it didn't go well.

"I see others getting what seems like dozens of people engaging with their posts. Forty-seven likes, fifty-two comments. Posts that must get thousands of impressions. I'm lucky if I can get one hundred people to see my posts. My top post this week had 134 views, with eight likes, and four comments. That was my best post. Some of my posts get next to no engagement at all!" Alex was clearly frustrated with his lack of traction on LinkedIn.

"It's only been two weeks, Alex," Carolina consoled him. "Be patient."

"I just don't know what I'm doing wrong."

"You are smart. I know you will learn and get great at it." Another reassuring affirmation from his wife. "In the meantime, you have managed to set up two workshops where you have filled the room with potential clients. You are a great speaker and presenter. But not everything will come easy."

"The worst of it all was that one comment I received on that post," Alex said, rolling his eyes.

"There are trolls on social media. Just ignore them."

"But this wasn't a complete stranger."

"Who was it?"

"Rob."

"Rob Langley? From DelTech?"

"Yup, that Rob."

"What did he comment?"

"I had written a post about the five characteristics of a highly innovative team. Rob wrote a snarky comment mocking me."

"What did he write?"

"Something like, 'too bad you walked away from a team with all five of those characteristics. I see you are a team of one now. Hope that's working out for you.'"

"What a jerk. If it was someone you respected, that is one thing. But it's Rob. Ignore him."

"Want to know what bothers me the most? I used to be like Rob. Driven, cocky, arrogant."

"Driven, yes. Cocky and arrogant, no," Carolina corrected Alex. "You both have a drive to work hard and are high achievers, but that is where the similarities end. Trust me, in no other way are you like Rob Langley."

Alex and Rob had been quite close up until the DelTech family summer get together six years ago. It was there that Alex noticed Rob's arrogant side. The company had rented a huge park to accommodate the two hundred attendees of employees and their families. Several games and activities were planned to help adults as well as children enjoy their time and create a family friendly culture. "Family friendly" it was not, thanks to Rob.

The games and activities became a competition, with Rob wanting him and his children to be the winners. Whether through pushing, shoving, or outright cheating, Rob and his two sons ended up taking home first prize, while making several enemies in the process. Martin, six at the time, took an elbow to the ribs from Rob's nine-year-old son on the monkey bars. Luckily, he was not badly hurt when he fell.

What really got under Alex's skin was seeing Rob give his son a high-five after the incident. What kind of a person encourages and celebrates that type of behavior in their child?

Other kids went home crying. Other DelTech employees had it rubbed in their face at work on Monday by Rob bragging about the big win. Alex quickly distanced himself from Rob from that point on.

"I guess I'm just struggling with the idea of not being a raving success already with Align. Just feeling sorry for myself. I'll get past this." Alex was saying this as much for his own benefit as he was for Carolina.

He was used to things coming easy for him. Ever since he started his own company, he was suddenly a beginner in so many areas. Luckily, he loved to learn. Some things just take longer to master than others.

As the weeks went on, Alex put the comment from Rob behind him. He hosted two different paid workshops that exposed him to several new potential clients. He loved the energy of live workshops, wowing the participants with his great presentations, facilitating breakout sessions where people fed off each other's ideas, and leaving people motivated with new tools and strategies they could implement within their teams. He delivered a great deal of value in his workshops. Many participants saw him as a trusted expert and would eventually reach out to ask for his help.

Yes, the workshops would prove to be a great lead generator for Alex as time went on.

As for LinkedIn, Alex saw some slow improvement. A few new people started to engage with his posts and connect with him. One person in particular, Sarah Emerson, was another consultant. Much like Charles Redding, Sarah seemed to be a few years ahead of Alex. She had over twelve thousand followers on LinkedIn and was getting a lot of engagement on her posts.

Alex asked if they could have a virtual coffee to chat and talk about LinkedIn engagement. Much like Charles, Sarah was more than happy to talk and share her tips.

She taught Alex so much about the fundamentals of LinkedIn.

- ✔ How to structure your post with a hook at the beginning to draw people in and leaving them wanting to read more.
- ✔ How to ensure you are giving away value in the meat of your post.
- ✔ How to end your post with a call to engagement.

When it came to the meat of the post—the value— Sarah liked to use lists. "People love lists," she insisted. "Lists of books people should read. Lists of mistakes you have made other people should avoid. Lists of your favorite quotes on a specific subject. Lists of your top tips or strategies you have learned in the past year. Lists of the top skills you would like to master." It seemed like Sarah had an endless content generation engine to draw from.

The call to engagement was important to entice people to add their insights to your post. "Ask a question that will be sure to spark some conversation in the comments," she explained.

It all made perfect sense. And Alex could see now that this format was used by so many others on LinkedIn. It was generating a lot of engagement.

"But posting good content is only one piece of the puzzle," Sarah added. "You also need to make sure you are engaging in the comments. Both on your own posts and other people's. Whenever someone makes a comment on your post, respond to it. But make sure you do it in a conversational way. Ask them a question, ask them for examples. Your goal should be for people to get value from your posts whether it is from the content of the post itself, or the insightful conversations that happen in the comments. Make that happen."

"What about when I am commenting on other people's posts?"

"Well, there are two parts to this." Sarah held up her index finger indicating she was about to make her first point. "First, make sure you are mostly only commenting on posts that are relevant to the topics you post about. You want to be seen as an expert on customer-centricity, innovation, and growth strategy. Search for people, posts, and groups around those topics. Don't just comment on any and every post you see that interests you. Don't just connect with anyone. Connect with people you can learn from or people who may be potential clients in the future. Be intentional."

That one hit home. Alex had not been applying any strategy to who he connected with on LinkedIn or what posts he was engaging with. It made so much sense to niche down, just like Mikaela had advised him to do with his website.

"Then," Sarah held up another finger, indicating point number two was coming, "make sure when you do comment on a post, you are adding value. Give insightful tips. Ask insightful questions. Help that person by making the comments section on their posts a great place for people to learn. They will love you for it and will likely want to return the favor."

"This has been terrific advice, Sarah." Alex had two pages full of notes and was now full of ideas on how he would approach LinkedIn moving forward.

"One final thing," Sarah added.

"What's that?"

"I found that posting at the same time every morning works well for me. It's like people come to expect it. Plus, every new person I connect with, I let them know that I post every morning at 8:00 a.m. This consistency has helped boost the engagement on my posts."

"You post every day at 8:00 a.m.?" Alex said, repeating what she had just told him. Again, he did not have any strategy about how often or when he was posting on LinkedIn. He could see now that he had just been throwing things at the wall and hoping something would stick.

"Yes, but I don't write a new post each morning. I write a week's worth of posts all at once and then use a scheduling tool to have them come out each morning at eight. Then, I just show up with my coffee each morning and respond to the comments."

Again, Alex was impressed with the thought that had gone into Sarah's strategy. It would have taken him weeks, or maybe months, to figure all of this out on his own. "And with your endless ideas for content combined with your consistent post format you use, I guess it doesn't take you too long to write a week's worth of posts."

"It took me time to get into a good rhythm. Now I have it down to about thirty minutes."

Alex and Sarah signed off the video call equally happy. Alex was delighted to have gathered so much knowledge. Sarah told Alex how pleased she was to be able to help someone out who was in the same position she was a few years ago.

At that point in time, Alex had 784 connections on LinkedIn and was averaging around 200 impressions on his posts. Sarah guaranteed him that both of those numbers would rise dramatically if he consistently followed her strategy.

They agreed to check in with each other in a few months so Alex could update her on his journey.

Again, the message from Pastor Johnson's sermon that following Sunday seemed to be speaking directly to Alex.

"Do nothing out of selfish ambition or vain conceit. Rather, in humility value others above yourselves." Wise words from the apostle Paul in the book of Philippians.

Alex reflected on Charles and Sarah. Their willingness to give him their time and advice. Their focus on adding value for others. It wasn't about them. It was about lifting up those around them.

It was at that point Alex vowed he would do the same for others. He would pay it forward whenever given the opportunity.

That Sunday afternoon, everything seemed right in the world as Alex, Carolina, and Martin had a nice meal with some close friends after church and then took an extended bike ride together through a trail leading to Martin's favorite park.

The world of DelTech and climbing the corporate ladder seemed miles away.

CHAPTER REFLECTION QUESTIONS

✔ What can you do to ensure you are finding joy in each day and embracing the journey?

✔ Do you have close family or friends that can provide support and motivation during the difficult times?

✔ How can you ensure you are in tune with your current or potential customers' needs, wants, and behaviors?

Chapter 6

"We are doing fine," Carolina said in her loving, supportive voice.

How was she always so optimistic and encouraging? Didn't she ever get stressed about finances or their future? Was this a trait passed down to her from her mother?

"We have trimmed our budget back to accommodate our lower income and it hasn't had any negative impact on us or our happiness. In fact, we were probably living too extravagantly before," she reasoned.

Alex knew she was right, but he hated the thought that his inability to bring in a higher income meant they had to cut back in certain areas. It's not like they were poor. But Alex had different expectations for how much money he would bring in through his new consulting venture.

After a quick scan of his calendar for the week, he could see he was right in the middle of what he called his "solopreneur consulting cycle."

At the start of each cycle, there was a tremendous amount of time and attention focused on marketing and sales initiatives—attend networking events and follow up on any leads from connections made, reach out to previous clients to check and see if they needed help in other areas, and prepare for and host workshops for businesses in the area to make some new connections and keep his name out there.

In the middle of the cycle, Alex was busy following up on the various leads through exploratory calls and meetings, scoping work, and sending proposals.

This is exactly what his week would consist of. He had three calls and two meetings lined up with five different companies this week to discuss their current challenges.

One call was with a previous client he did some consulting for a few months back. The other two calls were with business contacts he had met through LinkedIn. He had been posting regularly for five months straight. In that time, his posts were getting more attention, averaging over twelve hundred views each. Plus, Alex now had over three thousand connections. Even Sarah was impressed.

The two meetings were with companies that had sent people to one of his recent workshops about managing change in an innovative company. Alex thought it was his best workshop yet. He had found a perfect format for his events where he was able to deliver a lot of value, create a ton of energy in the room, and build trust with the participants.

He would open each workshop with a check in/ ice breaker by having each participant talk about themselves. Who are they? Why are that here? What do they want to learn? Then, he would throw in some fun questions like asking them to name their favorite movie as a child, or the most interesting place they have visited.

Once everyone was feeling comfortable and the ice was broken, he would follow a set formula for delivering each piece of learning content. Starting with an engaging story to capture the participants' attention, he would then deliver value through information sharing, and follow that up by facilitating a collaborative discussion about what this means for their business or industry. Rinse and repeat.

To wrap up each workshop, Alex would then facilitate another collaborative discussion about the next steps for the businesses in attendance, making sure to provide a call to action for each participant.

Alex had no new prospective clients through the various networking events he had attended lately. It was mostly the same people at each event, and he was considering dropping it as a sales and marketing tool. The workshops and LinkedIn avenues seemed to be paying better dividends.

The eventual fruits of his labours would then lead him to the next part of his cycle, which was delivering consulting engagements to the businesses that agreed to bring him on.

The pattern was one he had been through several times now. It was known. It was easily repeatable. He was getting into a groove.

Marketing and networking ➤ Exploratory sales calls ➤ Deliver consulting

Marketing and networking ➤ Exploratory sales calls ➤ Deliver consulting

Marketing and networking ➤ Exploratory sales calls ➤ Deliver consulting

But there was a problem.

Only the final portion of the cycle—deliver consulting—saw Alex getting paid for his time. Luckily, he was now attracting businesses that understood his worth and happily paid for the value they were getting from his consulting services.

The first two parts of the cycle were necessary for Alex to invest in since those efforts were what led to new consulting work. But when he was engaged in a consulting project with a business, he had to scale back on his sales and marketing efforts. He only had so much time.

The process was starting to become a predicament, a vicious cycle.

Sure, the process was working, but not nearly as well as Alex needed it to. It was bringing in new consulting work. But was it enough? Alex had been a full-time consultant for almost a complete year now, and, based on his earnings so far, he was projected to bring in $89,000 in year one. Not bad, but a far cry from his $165k salary, benefits, and bonuses he was receiving at DelTech.

"We are almost at the year mark," Alex reminded Carolina, "and I'm conflicted about whether to continue with Align. I did fine in year one, and I have enjoyed the challenge of starting my own business and everything I have learned, not to mention all the new people I have met."

"And you have your health back," Carolina added. It was true. Alex was down twenty-five pounds and felt better than he had in years. "And your anxiety is under control."

Alex was weaning off his medication. Not that being a solopreneur wasn't stressful, at times, but it was a different kind of stress. He was working for himself, not someone else. He couldn't quite explain it, but it was just different. A lighter load to carry.

"And you have been able to spend more time what Martin and me." Carolina was building a pretty strong case. She knew the alternative was Alex finding another corporate job and getting sucked back into the workaholic lifestyle he was living before.

"Well, if I'm going to stick with it, I need to figure out how to beat this cycle. Either I need to offload some of the sales and marketing work, or I need to create some more revenue streams." Alex's mind turned with ideas.

"Why not both?" Carolina suggested. That struck a chord with Alex.

A two-pronged strategy was soon developed. Step one was to find ways to effectively offload some sales and marketing work so he could spend more time performing paid consulting engagements. Step two was to find other ways to get paid other than simply trading his time for money. Alex loved the idea of getting paid for something he could build once and sell a thousand times. Recurring passive income was the ultimate goal. The ability to derive continuous revenue streams to help sustain a consultant through the dry periods removes a lot of pressure. So he could continue to service existing clients and not have to constantly chase after new ones.

To offload sales and marketing, Alex first ensured that he had tested and refined his processes. If these were going to be handed over to someone else, they needed to be easily repeatable and documented.

These tasks included:

- ✔ Identifying potential new businesses to connect with and sending an introductory email

- ✔ Responding to certain emails and contact requests that came in through his website or LinkedIn

- ✔ Scheduling introductory calls with prospective clients

- ✔ Handling the workshop scheduling and logistics

- ✔ Responding to any workshop registration questions or issues

Once the tasks were identified, and processes documented, Alex looked into several outsourcing options. There were full-scale agencies that came with their own software platforms and individual VAs (virtual assistants) that would take on designated tasks to help lighten the load.

At this point, he felt he could not justify paying for any of the higher-end outsourcing solutions, even if he would love to be in a position to do so in another year or two. Alex spoke with several VAs before deciding on one he felt comfortable with and confident in to take over his selected sales and marketing initiatives.

On average, taking these tasks off of his plate would save Alex around six to ten hours each week. For the $750 a month he would be paying the VA for this work, his plan would be to fill that time with either more consulting work or building assets he could sell.

SOLOPRENEUR LESSON—VIRTUAL ASSISTANTS

> ❯ Once you have established some processes, look to offload repeatable tasks, ones that are not a good fit for your strengths, or those that are not adding as much value for your time.

It took a few weeks to get the VA fully up to speed on performing the tasks in a manner that mimicked Alex's style and processes. They agreed to meet weekly at first to review the tasks, tweak the processes, and answer any questions. It became an effective and efficient meeting that eventually moved to a bi-weekly one as they both grew more comfortable with each other.

"I was skeptical at first, but this is working out well now that we have a good rhythm going," Alex reflected one night as he and Carolina sat on the sofa chatting before bed. "Thanks for encouraging me to document my processes. That made a huge difference."

"I'm not just a pretty face," Carolina answered.

With his new VA now in place and fully trained, Alex turned his attention to step two. But what assets should he build?

Through research and talking with other consultants, he discovered four approaches commonly taken:

1. Create a software platform or app that people pay a monthly or yearly fee to use.

2. Write a book that you can publish and sell in e-book, hardcopy, and even audio format.

3. Develop an online course that people purchase if they don't have the time or budget to work with you directly.

4. Create a podcast or newsletter where you can build up an audience and eventually sell advertising spots.

The idea of a software platform appealed to Alex. However, even though he had deep experience working in the tech industry with a background in innovation, he did not possess the coding skills required to build something himself. Besides, what would he build? Who could he partner with to build something? This was an idea he may examine again in the future if the right opportunity should arise.

What about a book? Some consultants he spoke to said that publishing a business book helped solidify their credibility as an expert in a certain area and in turn brought them more consulting engagements.

That appealed to Alex, but he would also want the book to be a source of revenue so he didn't have to rely so much on his consulting work. His goal was to diversify his revenue streams and spend less time trading his time for money. Would a book bring him closer to that goal?

How about an online course? Alex had taken many courses himself and found some were of great value while others were definitely not worth the money he paid. Could he create a course that would be of value to businesses?

A podcast or newsletter sounded like a fun challenge, but how long would it take him to build up a big enough audience for him to monetize it? Again, this would be more a long-term play that he could revisit in the future if and when he wanted to. Besides, he was already putting time into building an audience on LinkedIn. "Don't lose your focus. One audience building strategy at a time," he told himself.

Alex would need to spend some more time thinking about this before determining his next steps.

Over the next two months, the VA proved to be a great asset. Alex had created documents and instructional videos to help train the person on the tasks they were taking on. They continued to meet bi-weekly to review any questions, challenges, or concerns and continually developed new processes to make things as efficient as possible.

With new businesses being added to his pipeline without much of Alex's effort involved, he was now spending more time quoting and delivering consulting work. So far so good.

On LinkedIn, he was in a groove with templates for six different types of posts he found worked the best. He would routinely write the posts in advance, swapping in different tactics, learnings, and musings around innovation, scaling a business, customer-centricity, and strategy. He used a scheduling tool to have his posts come out at the same time each morning and would spend forty-five minutes engaging with people in the comments on his posts as well as posts from other people who wrote about similar topics.

His network was now up to almost four thousand people and his posts were averaging over fifteen hundred views each. More progress!

Alex enjoyed writing the posts. He was learning how to capture people's attention, whether it be with a thought-provoking question, a devil's advocate view on a certain topic, or statement that would leave the reader wanting to learn more. He had mastered the art of the hook. A year ago, Alex knew next to nothing about copywriting. Now people were commenting about the excellent writing in his posts. Some commenters requested his advice about how to write more effectively. That gave Alex a sense of pride and opened his mind a bit to the possibility of writing a book.

Perhaps it would be a fun challenge.

He could write a book using some of his most popular LinkedIn posts as the basis for the content, and then self publish it on Amazon. That would be a terrific learning experience and allow him to use the title "Author" in his bio on LinkedIn and his website. Instant credibility. How hard could it be?

As Alex would soon find out, writing and publishing a book were not terribly difficult. Writing, publishing, marketing, and promoting a *great* book was a different story, however.

Over the next two months, Alex took some of his most popular content from LinkedIn and turned it into a longer form book. In total, it was 117 pages of strategies and tactics around innovation. He lined up five different family members and friends to read the manuscript, asking them to point out any grammar or spelling errors and to provide general feedback. Of course, they all thought it was wonderful.

Each person found some mistakes he needed to correct, gave some opinions on some sentences that could be worded better, and applauded him for taking on this endeavour.

His cousin Susan, who graduated with an English major several years ago, gave him high praise. "Such a great read. Thanks so much for asking me to be a proofreader. Let me know when it's published and I'll tell all my friends."

If Susan thought it was great, then it must be. This book was going to be a huge success. Alex was already dreaming of the royalty payments he would be receiving from Amazon each month.

The entire process cost him zero dollars. He used family and friends to edit the book, and he designed his own book cover using Canva. Alex was proud of how fast he managed to put together the book and ready it for publication.

After learning how to properly format the book for both e-book and paperback release, determining the price, selecting the categories it would be listed under, and then creating his author page, Alex was ready to let the world know he was now an author.

"I am delighted to announce that today I have published a book to help businesses be more innovative. *Get Aligned With Innovation* is now available on Amazon. Check the link in the comments to grab your copy!"

His LinkedIn post received a great deal of engagement.

"Congrats, Alex!"

"Wow, that's terrific."

"Amazing."

There was plenty of praise for his latest project, but it certainly didn't translate into the type of sales numbers he had been dreaming of.

Alex could not wait to see the orders pouring in for his new book.

Only the orders didn't pour in at all.

At the end of the first week, Alex had sold exactly twenty-eight copies of his book. Sales would decline drastically each week moving forward. After six weeks, the sales had dried up like a raisin in the hot July sun. And so did Alex's over-inflated ego.

At least, he was now able to call himself an author, and there were benefits that came with being the author of a business book, even if it wasn't a bestseller. He could give copies of his book to prospective clients and could sell or give away copies of his book at his workshops.

"Still, I'd like to figure out how to write a book people would be excited to buy and read," Alex confessed to Carolina, his first book creating a whimper instead of the bang he had imagined.

"Well, with Align, you learned the most by talking to other consultants that were a few years ahead of you, right? So why not do the same with some authors?"

Duh. Why hadn't Alex thought of that? Of course, Carolina was right. Again. Rather than trying to do it all on his own, rather than learning through his own mistakes, why not learn from someone who had already taken a similar journey?

Alex appreciated her support. He also knew she enjoyed it when he bounced ideas off her and was happy to be contributing to the new life he was building. The look she gave him said it all—a warm smile and wink to let him know he could expect more support whenever he needed it.

Over the next few weeks, eager to get as much advice and insight as possible, Alex talked to all different types of authors—best-selling, independent, self-published, fiction, nonfiction. In all, Alex spoke to eight different people and collected a great deal of valuable information that would help him write, publish, and market his next book.

He was strongly advised, however, to hire a professional editor and experienced graphic designer. Ironically, these were precisely the two things Alex thought he'd be able to cut corners with on with his last book. Another lesson learned.

Apparently, a good editor would do much more than just correct any spelling or grammatical mistakes. They would help him with flow, readability, structure, format too. They would teach Alex how to capture the readers' attention at the beginning of each chapter. They would educate him on how to make the reader want to keep reading when they got to the end of a chapter, how to create that need for the reader to see what happens next. Yes, a good editor is worth their weight in gold, he was informed. He could now see the mistake he'd made by having only friends and family proofread his first book.

And it seems like the old adage is actually true, people do judge a book by its cover. Alex thought he did a fairly good job designing the cover for his last book. He could not have been more wrong.

"It looks okay, but it doesn't look like a real book. It looks like the author designed the cover himself. If that's what I think when I see it, others will too." Those are the exact words he heard from John Swinson, one of the authors he spoke with when Alex proudly showed him a copy of his last book.

His pride and smile faded quickly at hearing the feedback. It wasn't just the cover, John told him. A professional graphics designer would also know how to properly format the book. Alex had just saved his last manuscript as a PDF and uploaded it into Amazon.

"It's formatted like a college essay," John said. "You want it to look like a book, with nicely formatted chapters, proper spacing, and everything that makes a book look like a book." Alex's smile was now non-existent as he reflected on how much he didn't know about book publishing.

A completely separate set of advice he received was how to properly promote the book. What good is a great book if nobody knows about it? Apparently, this was something Alex failed to do entirely the first time around.

Alex felt like he earned an MBA in book marketing through everything he learned from the different authors he talked to. So much of this he wished he had known before writing his last book. It now made so much sense why he'd barely sold any copies. But now he knew, and he was ready to put a plan in place.

Starting his marketing as soon as possible, long before the book was published, was the main theme of most of the advice he'd received. How do you market a book that's not been published yet? Heck, he hadn't even written a single word!

Turns out, it was about leveraging other people in order to help amplify the promotion of the book when it would be finally released. It made sense now why he needed to start ASAP.

The three main strategies he would deploy looked like this:

Influencer Leverage

✔ Alex would make a list of one hundred influential people that would be ideal to read and help promote his book. People with a large following on social media. People who are respected as experts in the topic discussed in his book. People that have a senior level position in a company, like CEO or VP.

✔ Next, he would begin to follow these people on social media and engage with their content in an insightful way. He would post comments on their posts asking intelligent questions and/or contributing valuable insights of his own.

✔ Over the course of several weeks or months, Alex would finally reach out to the person directly, whether through private message or via email, and introduce himself. He would let them know he enjoyed their content. Hopefully, people would respond and strike up a conversation.

✔ Eventually, closer to the release of the book, Alex would let them know he was set to publish a new book soon and ask them if they would like to read the manuscript and provide a short review that could be printed on or just inside the cover.

✔ Out of the one hundred people, surely he would find ten to fifteen that would be happy to do so, especially since he would be taking the time to first earn their respect and build a relationship.

✔ When the book was published, he would send them each a signed copy. If each of them posted on social media about his book, including a picture of the physical copy, this would help to generate interest from an audience of people that Alex wouldn't typically have access to directly.

Podcasts

✔ Similar to leveraging influential people, Alex would take parallel approach and target specific podcasts that would be ideal for him to appear on as a guest to discuss his book.

✔ He would make a list of the top one hundred podcasts that would already have a captive audience interested in the book's subject.

✔ He would listen to various episodes of the podcasts to get a feel for the host's style and note a few episodes that he enjoyed.

✔ The same approach would be taken to follow the hosts on social media, engage with their content, and eventually build a relationship after reaching out directly at the right point in time.

✔ Alex would then let the hosts know about his upcoming book and mention that he would love to be a guest on their show.

✔ Podcasts were always looking for interesting guests that their audience would enjoy, so he would be sure to include a list of intriguing questions they should ask him on the show.

✔ His goal was to have fifty podcast interviews lined up by the time the book was released. Again, this would help expose him and his book to an audience of people he would otherwise not be able to easily tap into.

LinkedIn

✔ With Alex becoming more and more proficient at building his own audience on LinkedIn, he would leverage this to help build anticipation about his upcoming book.

- ✔ People love to be brought along for the ride when you are building or creating something. Alex would inform his connections, through a post, that he was excited to be writing a new book. To create suspense, he would not immediately reveal its exact topic.

- ✔ Every so often, maybe once every other week, Alex would write a post updating everyone about his progress. How far along was he in his writing? What obstacles or challenges was he running into? What was he learning along the way?

- ✔ By the time the book would be ready to release, everyone in his network would be well aware that it was coming and hopefully intrigued to purchase and read it since they would feel as though they were a part of the writing journey.

The only thing left for Alex to do was write the book. No big deal, right? Well, this was another area where he had a ton to learn.

SOLOPRENEUR LESSON—BOOK STRATEGY

The three things you want to do well with any book:

- ❯ Editing
- ❯ Design
- ❯ Promotion

Take the lessons Alex learned and put a strategy in place when writing a book to help it look, read, and sell better.

"Writing a book is like building a house." This time it was Alicia Ross giving Alex the advice. Alicia had written four best-selling books and was another person Alex was surprised had given him the time of day to sit and chat. "First, you need your main theme of the book. I understand you will be writing a nonfiction business book, correct?"

"That's right."

"What is the theme of your book? Why should people read it?"

"I'll be giving them a structure for building a more customer-centric and innovative business."

"That's the structure and content of your book, but why should a business owner or leader read your book?"

"So their business will be more customer-centric and innovative!" Alex thought this was obvious from his last response.

"But why is that important?"

He now saw Alicia's point.

"Remember, you want people to want to read your book. What will reading your book do for them? More specifically, what will having a more customer-centric and innovative company do for them?"

"By being more customer-centric they will have better insights into their customers, why they purchase their products and services." Alex, already anticipating her next question about why that is important, added, "This will allow them to create strategies and tactics to better market and sell to those customers and create a better customer experience using their product and service." Another WHY question was coming. "So they can ensure they are building a flock or customers who want to come back and do business over and over. Loyal customers. People that love their brand and love doing business with them."

"Great! So where does the innovation part fit in?"

"People change fast. Trends come and go. New technologies emerge. Markets evolve. Companies need to be innovative and constantly use the customer-centric insights they are gaining to find new and better ways to serve their customers. Plus, when they have a culture of innovation, it makes for a better place to work for the employees. People are much more excited to come to a place to work when their creativity is encouraged, where they get to participate in brainstorming sessions and test out new ideas." Alex could see some themes emerging.

"It sounds like business owners or executives should read your book so they can turn indifferent customers and employees into raving fans of their business."

Alex's jaw just about hit the floor. Alicia took the basic idea for the content of his book and flipped it to look at it through the eyes of the reader. The idea of turning indifferent customers and employees into fans sounded like an incredible theme for a book.

"That sure sounds a lot sexier than giving them a structure for building a more customer-centric and innovative business." Alex was still amazed at how much more appealing a book can look just by changing the way it's positioned.

"So it sounds like you have your foundation."

"We're building a house, you said. So, what comes next?"

"Now you need your structure. Your main points are like the rooms of the house, and they translate into the book's chapters."

"This is where I already have some good content outlined. I have several strategies and tactics for how a business can be more customer-centric and innovative." Alex was proud knowing he had done something right already.

"Great, then comes the finer details of the house to make it look nice. The floors, the windows, the light fixtures."

"And how does that translate in the book? What's the equivalent of flooring, windows, and lights?" Alex was intrigued with this metaphor.

"Your writing. Your voice. The stories you use to draw in readers and capture their attention. The way you make the strategies and tactics relatable to them and their business so they feel motivated to implement them."

"Sounds like this is where a good editor will help me." Alex was getting it now.

"Exactly." Alicia was pleased to see Alex was setting himself up for success and preparing himself to write a good book. "Keep in touch and let me know how it goes."

After several valuable discussions, there was a lot of information to digest. But first things first. Alex would need to decide whether he would go the traditional publishing route. This would require using an agent to find him a publisher that would pay for his manuscript. Or maybe he would self-publish.

His takeaway from the various conversations he'd had was that there were pros and cons to both possibilities. The traditional publishing route typically comes with more cache for your book, especially if you land a deal with a big-name publisher. But Alex would not control the rights to his book, meaning he would stand to make less money off each copy sold. Also, with so many books being purchased online nowadays, did you really need a publisher to release your book on a site like Amazon? Alex had gone through that process already with his last book and discovered the simplicity of it.

Alex decided if he was going to write another book, he would stick with the self-publishing route. It may mean a little less cache behind the book, but he was willing to put the work in to market it. After speaking to so many authors and hearing their perspectives, learning from their mistakes, and writing down their advice, Alex now had a much better idea what it was going to take to write, publish, and market a book people would want to read.

It seemed daunting.

Could he do it? Did he have the time? The virtual assistant certainly was helping lighten his load by taking several administrative tasks off his plate. He was also getting more efficient at preparing for and delivering workshops. Even his consulting engagements were taking less of his time as he had continually found better and faster ways to deliver the same high-quality results.

But that extra time he had found was being spent with Carolina and Martin. Did he really want to use that time properly writing and marketing a book instead?

Again, Alex found himself conflicted and at a crossroads. And again, it was a divine intervention that helped him decide what to do. At least, Alex's ego centered interpretation of another Sunday morning message.

"Thus says the Lord, the God of Israel, 'Write all the words which I have spoken to you in a book,'" Pastor

Johnson exclaimed in his sermon that week. He was reading from the Book of Jeremiah.

The theme of his talk was centered around the Bible being God's word. Or "God breathed" as Pastor Johnson put it.

But it inspired Alex. Everything he learned through his many years at DelTech and his first year and three months as a solo consultant should be written into a book. Not like his last book, thrown together quickly from LinkedIn posts. But a real book, with the intent of helping business owners and senior executives build a better company.

The decision was made that Sunday morning. And it changed everything.

CHAPTER REFLECTION QUESTIONS

- ✔ Are you leveraging social media to help create an identity and awareness of your brand?

- ✔ What tasks are you performing that can be easily documented and delegated to someone like a virtual assistant?

- ✔ What opportunities do you have to create assets you can sell so that you are not relying solely on selling your time for money?

Chapter 7

"Are you coming to my hockey game tonight? Or are you staying home to 'work on your book'?" Martin flourished his request with finger quotes and an eye roll, and Alex could see how his son felt about his dad possibly missing another one of his hockey games.

Alex was now a few months into his writing, and it was as if things had come full circle.

Right before leaving DelTech, Alex was in a constant state of disappointing both Martin and Carolina. Working long hours, skipping out on family time, putting his work first.

Here he was again. With the burning desire to do something great, but with the same cost for his family.

Over the past six months, consumed in his business, he had fallen back into many old habits. Between facilitating his workshops that were ever growing in popularity, working with his consulting clients, posting and engaging on LinkedIn, checking in with his virtual assistant, and now researching and writing his new book, the old Alex had slowly returned.

Gone was the Alex who was taking regular walks, spa retreats, and date nights with his wife. Gone was the Alex who was spending more time with his son; fishing, hiking, school trips, and, of course, watching his hockey games.

Back was workaholic Alex, the healthy eating and exercise habits gone. Back was the Alex with a drive and desire overly focused on his next goal. Back was the tension in the Green household.

"What time is the game?" Alex asked.

"I told you already. 7:30." Martin looked frustrated.

"I am just putting the finishing touches on this chapter. I will be there." Even Alex wondered if it was an empty promise.

"They're playing the Rangers tonight. He really wants you to be there," Carolina whispered softly in his ear. This was more than just a nudge for Alex to attend the game. This was a reminder of how much his son needed his love and attention.

"I promise I will be there." Alex was hoping to appease both Carolina and Martin. He needed them to back off and give him space to continue his writing. He was in a groove, and when a writer is in a groove, time stands still. The ideas are abundant, the words flow. For Alex, the creativity tap was opened to its full capacity, and the writing rushed out of him. He could see the book taking its final shape. He had been working hard on it. All the extra hours he was putting in would soon pay off.

That's when the door to his office slammed shut, startling Alex as he nearly jumped out of his seat, the tiny hairs on the back of his neck suddenly standing at attention. It was Carolina. She had entered the office and closed the door to be alone with Alex. The look on her face told him everything he needed to know about what she was thinking. He knew she was not impressed.

"I said I promise I will make it to the game." Alex was attempting to calm her down, speaking in a soft but desperate voice, hoping Martin would not hear their conversation.

"Listen, I have supported you through every step of this journey." Her fiery Chilean side had definitely been triggered. She too was speaking softly, but it was a stern whisper. The look on her face indicated her displeasure in her husband. "We did not go through this whole life transition just to have you go back to being a workaholic."

"I know, I know."

"I'm leaving now to take Martin to his game. Don't disappoint us." That last line was delivered with an extra harsh look. Alex got the message. With that, Carolina opened the door to the office, put a smile on her face and said, "Bye, my love, we will see you soon." That line was for Martin.

Stunned by the events, Alex sat quietly in his chair for a few minutes, now alone in the house. He had done it again. Carolina was right, she had been extremely supportive throughout this journey. Almost unbelievably so. Had he taken advantage of it? Did he take it for granted? It sure seemed like he had pushed her past her limits.

But Alex was so close. The book was almost done. Didn't she understand? Just a little longer and he would have it completed.

He turned back to his computer screen to focus on the manuscript again. Within minutes, he was lost in his writing. Back in the groove.

Time was standing still for Alex, yet he didn't consider how at that very moment each second was passing achingly slow for Martin and Carolina, who would sit wondering whether he would make it to the game or not, some of the parents asking of his whereabouts, Carolina too loving to say anything negative about her husband, barely even able to admit to herself that he was yet again choosing his work over his family. But would Martin be able to hold it in? Or would he express his disappointment in his father to one of his teammates? Would he be able to concentrate on the game, or would he be devoting his attention to scanning the bleachers for Alex, desperately hoping he would make it to the game?

At the midpoint of the third period, with Martin's team down 3-2, Alex walked into the arena. Carolina saw him first. She smiled, then let out a large sigh of relief. As if she had not been looking forward to the conversation on the ride home after the game, trying to defend him to Martin.

Alex made his way through the crowd and found his seat beside his wife. That's when Martin spotted him. He beamed with pride and excitement. His dad had made it in time to watch the most crucial part of the game. Martin seemed to find a little extra jump in his step.

The game remained at 3-2 as both teams made some terrific plays at both ends of the ice. The crowd was kept on the edge of their seats as the goalies were putting on a clinic for how to make the most acrobatic saves on what looked like sure goals.

With just under two minutes left to play, Martin's coach decided to pull the goalie and put an extra skater on the ice. It was a common tactic used by a team that desperately needed a goal to tie the game. Get control of the puck, use the extra skater to your advantage, find the open player, and, hopefully, set him up for a goal. But lose the puck to the other team and you risk the chance of them scoring an easy goal into your empty net, kissing goodbye any chance at tying the game.

Martin was the extra skater his coach elected to put on the ice with the goalie pulled. Alex knew how he felt. Adrenaline seemed to be running through his veins. His dad was in the stands watching. The game was on the line. These were the situations Alex loved to be in during his glory days. He could tell Martin thrived on it as well.

For the first thirty seconds, Martin's team controlled the puck. They swiftly passed it around in the offensive zone, trying to find an open player in a quality scoring position. A few different times, they found opportunities to score, but, again, the Ranger's goalie turned them aside.

Then, their worst fear transpired. One of the Ranger players stole the puck. They raced out of their end towards center ice with the puck on their stick. Martin was in quick pursuit. He knew he could not let them get close enough for an easy shot into the open net.

Just as the puck carrier passed center ice, Martin caught up to him. Sensing Martin, the player took a long-range shot, hoping to guide the puck down the ice into the empty net.

The crowd held their breath as they watched the puck slide down the ice, getting closer and closer to the goal. Carolina squeezed Alex's knee with her right hand. "No, no, no!" she shouted.

Just as the puck was about the enter the goal, Martin caught up to it and pulled it onto his stick. The crowd let out a collective gasp. He had just saved his team from going down 4-2. Alex grinned and squeezed Carolina's hand. Watching his son make such a great defensive play was a proud moment for him.

Now with only twenty-eight seconds left on the clock, Martin turned and rushed the puck up the ice. Once he was out of his own end, he passed it to one of his open teammates waiting at the Ranger's blue line. The puck was now back in the Ranger's end and Martin's team had control.

After catching his breath, Martin raced for the net and slapped his stick on the ice letting his teammate know he was open. With a quick and accurate pass from one his defensemen, the puck found him now streaking at full speed towards the goalie. Using a quick twist of his wrists, he shot the puck towards the top corner of the net on the blocker side.

The Ranger's goalie was one of the best in the league. He had already stopped Martin at least four times this game. But not this time. The shot was too fast and it sailed into the net to tie the game at three with five second left. The crowd erupted. First a great play by his son at one end of the ice to save a goal, now a terrific last second goal to tie the game at the other end of the ice. Alex's face beamed. Memories of his own heroics from the championship game so many years ago flashed through his mind.

Being a regular season game, it ended in a tie. Overtime was only for the playoffs. Martin was the hero of the night. With his last second heroics to tie the game, his team remained in first place.

Martin could not have been smiling any wider. Was it because of the goal? Or was it because his dad had been there to see it and cheer him on? Would he have scored if Alex was not there? Perhaps his dad was his lucky charm.

Alex had forgotten how much he loved watching Martin play. He vowed to himself to find a better balance. He would start getting back into the habits that saw him feeling like a better father and husband. He owed it to Martin and Carolina.

With the manuscript almost finished, Alex implemented a much more flexible schedule that prioritized time with his wife and son. A routine was created with meaningful and quality time set aside a few times each week to spend with Carolina and Martin. His writing times were more focused. He removed all distractions and dedicated sixty-minute slots to write.

This worked wonders. Not only was he getting back on track with his family, but he found his writing sessions to be much more productive. He was creating great habits.

With the manuscript now finished and in the hands of his editor, Alex was ramping up his marketing efforts. He had connected with over three hundred new people perfectly suited to help promote the book. There were podcasters, bloggers, social media influencers, journalists, business owners, CEOs, and other executives.

Twelve people agreed to write testimonials that would appear on or inside the book. Twenty-six podcasts had agreed to have him on as a guest. Seven bloggers were ready to write about the book. Nine bookstores would sell copies of his book on consignment. Those were just the people who had responded, so far. There were still dozens of people he hadn't heard back from yet.

Alex had also been creating buzz surrounding the book via LinkedIn, teasing his audience with some of the content and updating them on his writing journey. People were starting to ask how they could pre-order a copy. This was a good sign.

After the final editing, off the book went to the graphics company for formatting and a cover design. Alex was a bit overwhelmed with all the choices and decisions for the cover. There were three different options he liked. But which one was best? After asking several family members and close friends, he decided to seek the advice of his followers on LinkedIn, which was now up to over 8,100 and growing fast. But this tactic for choosing the best book cover didn't help at all!

He posted his three favorite cover designs and received way too many opinions on why each one was the right choice. There was no clear winner.

Alex went with his gut and chose the one that most caught his eye.

The time had arrived. The book was ready. All the hard work was finally about to pay off.

Unlike his first book, this one was met with a large group of people eagerly awaiting its release. Signed copies were mailed to over forty people the week of publication.

By Alex's standards, this book was a huge success. It quickly hit best-seller status in a few different categories on Amazon. The attention he had been creating leading up to the release was working. With each blog post about the book, more sales came in. With each podcast appearance, more sales came in. With each social media post by people receiving their signed copy and praising Alex and his book, more sales came in too.

Alex had created both more attention for his consulting business, plus two new revenue streams. The first revenue stream was from the book sales themselves. It would take a bit for him to make enough money to cover the costs for the editor and graphics design, but, eventually, the rest would be pure profit.

The other revenue stream it created for Alex was in the form of speaking engagements. People had seen the posts about the book and heard Alex on various podcasts, and he was now starting to get requests to speak at different events.

Some events offered to pay. These were great. He could easily take a lot of the content he used in his workshops and book and turn them into keynote speeches. Some events did not offer to pay, but allowed him to bring copies of his books to sell.

Alex carefully considered which events would put him in front of the right audiences.

With the book, the podcasts, the blogs, and now the speaking engagements, more companies were reaching out to him about his consulting services. There were so many emails and direct messages coming in that Alex almost missed a message from Rob Langley on LinkedIn.

"I see you are a writer now. I wonder how much more money you would be making if you had just stayed at DelTech. Good luck with your book."

What a backhanded compliment!

Alex had to remind himself that the people who hate on you were usually those who couldn't get over you not conforming to their self-determined expectations. Rob was still with DelTech. He was still a Vice President. He was likely still a workaholic and caught up in the hustle culture lifestyle that burned Alex out. He likely believed this is what everyone was supposed to do. Rob probably hated the fact Alex got out and wasn't following the same script.

The message he sent was more a reflection of him, than it was of Alex. Poor Rob.

There would always be naysayers like Rob. Alex would learn to ignore them as best as he could. For every negative comment, Alex was receiving a slew of congratulations and well wishes. He was riding an all-time high.

But he was also at a critical junction with Align. With the success of the book, now what?

"Should I try to scale my consulting business, bring on a partner, some employees? I could make it into a full-scale consulting agency. Or do I stay as a solopreneur and build more of a personal brand? Maybe I continue writing books, do more speaking engagements?" Alex's mind was overwhelmed with ideas and what steps to take next.

"Here is my favorite answer to those types of questions," Charles Redding said. They had agreed to chat and catch up since it had been over a year since they last talked. "It depends." Charles was smiling as he said it.

"That does seem to be a favorite answer of yours. I remember you telling me when we first met that I was smart to seek advice from others, but I needed to figure out what would work best for me. What does this next step depend on?" Alex was curious to hear what Charles had to say.

Charles took a sip of his coffee and sat back slowly. He looked up at Alex and said calmly, "What do you want?"

"Revenue wise?"

"I mean, what do you want? For you. For your family. Do you want to spend the next five years building a business, hiring and training employees,

DENNIS GEELEN ——— THE ACCIDENTAL SOLOPRENEUR

defining and implementing processes? Maybe you do. Maybe that excites you. You do have a corporate background."

"Yes, but I walked away from that life."

"Maybe what you want is to continue to build a lifestyle more suited to spending quality time with your lovely wife and son." Charles just let that statement hang in the air.

SOLOPRENEUR LESSON—SCALING OPTIONS

At some point, you may be in a position to scale your business.

❯ Do you want to create a bigger company with employees?

❯ Or do you want to continue to invest in growing your personal brand?

Start by thinking about the lifestyle you want for yourself and go from there.

Alex sat back. He had been laser focused on building. Building his brand, building his business, writing his book. He hadn't been focused at all on building a lifestyle. Sure, his health was better, and he had periods over the past few years where he had been able to spend more time with

Carolina and Martin. But was that by design, or just a consequence of slow periods in his business? He knew the answer.

"Let's say I want to focus on building the lifestyle I want. Couldn't that happen by scaling the consulting business up to the point where it runs itself?"

"It could, but it may take you five or even ten years to get to that point. That's if you do it right and you actually do get to that point. A lot of business founders end up creating a full-time job for themselves. Or worse, the business is so dependant on them that they have to put in sixty or even eighty hours a week to keep it going. Have you ever built a business from scratch before?"

"No, but I had never been a solo consultant before or written a book before, either."

"Did you make a lot of mistakes along the way before you started figuring things out?"

"Tons of mistakes. Luckily, I enjoyed the journey of learning."

"Yes, but this time it would be with other people's jobs and livelihood at risk, not just yours. Are you willing to make a bunch of mistakes and then hope you figure it out? To the point where you could some day step back from the business and reap the rewards?" Charles was doing a good job of asking questions without giving his opinion.

"Let's talk about the alternative for a minute. What if I stay a solopreneur? How would I design a lifestyle where I can spend quality time with my family and not have to be consulting and speaking on a regular basis?"

"Well, you have created one asset that you can now sell over and over."

"My book."

"Right. What other assets can you build that can continue to create a passive income?" Charles was pressing Alex to think deeper.

"I could write more books."

"Sure, and you probably should, eventually. But how else can you leverage the book you just wrote? Can you build some more assets based on the book, some resources you can create once and sell over and over?" Charles was really probing now.

"Like an online course?"

"That's one option. Or any tools or resources that could go along with the book. Like cheat sheets or 'How To' guides. Of course, you would need to do some market research to see where there is a need. Find out from the people reading your book what would add the most value."

SOLOPRENEUR LESSON— LEVERAGING YOUR BOOK

- ❯ A book can be leveraged to create more assets that go along with it.
- ❯ Do some market research and determine other ways that you can leverage and monetize your book.

"That's smart," Alex replied. "Leverage the current book by building more assets that generate passive recurring revenue, and then go on to write a new book in a year or two. Rinse and repeat."

"If that interests you and if you think that would be a better way to create the lifestyle you want," Charles added.

Alex had a lot to think about. The idea of building Align into a larger consulting company sounded exciting. He had heard of many founders who scaled their business and then exited with a nice sum of money once they sold to a larger firm.

But how long would that take? Could he even do it? Did he really want to do it?

The idea of creating more digital assets he could build once and sell repeatedly also sounded exciting. He liked the idea of generating more passive recurring income. Plus, it seemed like it would be a better fit for the lifestyle he was trying to create for his family.

He was reminded of what Pastor Johnson said to him the previous year when they met. "Your real happiness lies in enjoying the daily activities you do that bring you joy. Learn to find and attach your joy to what you are doing each day."

Alex was intent on creating a life where he enjoyed each day. The problem was that Alex was his own worst enemy. He had no intention of having his book take over his life for several months. He didn't anticipate it impacting his relationships with Carolina and Martin. But it did. Was this propensity to allow his work to overwhelm him in his DNA? Was he a workaholic just looking for the next project to dive into headfirst? How could he guard himself against this?

Perhaps it was time to pay another visit to Pastor Johnson.

"I'm so glad to have you come back for another chat," the pastor said, greeting Alex as he came into his office. "You seem out of breath."

"I walked here," Alex said between heavy breaths. This was his chance to walk at a quick pace and burn calories. He never would have walked a few miles for a meeting in the past. That would have been a chance to drive his beloved Tesla, the car that now sat in the garage unused. How long had it been since he'd had it serviced?

"Good for you. And I see you have stuck it out and really made something out of your business." The last time he came to visit Pastor Johnson, Alex was going through a rough period of self-doubt. It was his chat with the pastor that spurred him to persevere. It felt like decades ago.

"Yes, I can't thank you enough. Our last visit helped me get through the challenges I was facing at the time. In fact, it probably saved me from jumping back into another corporate job and getting back onto the fast track to another anxiety attack." The anxiety attack also seemed like a lifetime ago.

"So, what brings you here this time around?"

"I'm looking for a different kind of advice. I was at a critical juncture, wondering what to do with my business, and I have sorted that out, I think." Alex was still not one hundred percent certain. "But I know whatever path I go down, I need to be much better at not letting my work consume me. What does the Bible say about being a workaholic?"

"The Bible has a lot to say about work." Pastor Johnson chuckled. "But perhaps telling you a bit about my own story might help you the most."

"What do you mean? What's your story?"

"Let me start by saying that I think I can relate to you and your workaholic personality quite a bit. Did you know that before coming here to be the lead pastor of this church seven years ago, I was on the brink of a panic attack myself?"

"Why? What happened?" Alex was quite intrigued to hear his story.

"Well, I was a young and ambitious man of God, out to save the world as fast as I could. It started with one church where I worked passionately to grow it from a congregation of three hundred to eight hundred. We had to renovate the church twice to fit in all the new people coming out each Sunday. Then we decided we needed more locations to serve more people. So we expanded. After ten years of growing and expanding, I found myself in charge of four different locations, preaching multiple times a week, and running myself into the ground."

"I had no idea." Alex was surprised.

"Yes, I thought I was doing the right thing. Reaching more people, giving more of myself. But my relationship with my wife suffered. I was barely being a father to my two daughters. But I was so passionate about building and growing and teaching and equipping. I couldn't help myself."

"So, what happened?"

"My wife talked some sense into me. She helped me realize I was doing a much better job of spreading God's love when I was able to give more of myself to less people. It had reached a point where I was no longer building relationships with my congregation and impacting their lives through one-on-one conversations. I didn't have time for that. I was too busy trying to preach to thousands of people each week while not spending any personal time with any of them."

"What did you do?"

"I decided not to let my quest for more distract me from the beauty of enough." He paused to let that sink in. The meaning in that statement caught Alex's attention. Was Alex missing out on the beauty of enough? Paster Johnson continued, "I realized there is much more beauty to be found in genuinely impacting a few people's lives rather than barely scratching the surface with thousands. So, I stepped down as lead pastor of the mega church I was leading. I wanted to get back to being someone of impact on a smaller scale. I wanted to be a better husband and father. I came here. And I put boundaries in place to not allow myself to be tempted to turn this place into a mega church too!" With that, Pastor Johnson let out a laugh. He knew he was just like Alex in that regard and had to protect himself from those same temptations.

"Wow. I had no idea. Has it been tough to fight the temptations to go back to your old ways?"

"In the beginning, yes. I went from going a thousand miles an hour to working at a normal pace and spending more time with my family. It was a huge adjustment at first, and I was regularly tempted to attempt something on a grander scale. It was in my blood. But, over time, as I resisted and continued to put boundaries in place, I was able to find the beauty in enough."

"'The beauty in enough.' I love it," Alex said.

"You will, if you can get there too."

"I will."

CHAPTER REFLECTION QUESTIONS

- ✔ Have you thought about how you might scale your business? What would that look like for you?

- ✔ What can you do to ensure you are not tempted to have your business take over your life? What boundaries can you put in place to prevent this?

- ✔ What does "enough" look like for you?

Chapter 8

"I can honestly say this was not the life I was trying to design for myself. When I think back to the path I was on just a few years ago, I was headed in an entirely different direction. But here I am now, and I couldn't be happier," Alex reflected.

"Sure, life isn't perfect. Carolina and I still have the odd disagreement about pace and timeliness, but nothing like the friction between us in the past. Boy, was that something that used to cause a lot of tension, and, admittedly, I was the one who had it all backwards.

"Martin, our now fifteen-year-old son, who seems like he's going on eighteen, still loves to get under my skin by trying to stay up as late as possible playing video games, only to then attempt to sleep in half of the next day. But I'm spending time with him, getting to be a dad, being a role model. Not like I was before."

Alex was being interviewed on a podcast, promoting the release of his latest book. As the host asked him how his life had changed since leaving the corporate world and starting his own consulting practice, Align, Alex was caught up in a moment of nostalgia.

"Life isn't perfect, but perfection wasn't the goal," Alex continued.

"What was your goal when you left your corporate job?"

"To be honest, in the beginning I wasn't sure. I just knew something needed to change. But then it became clear. The goal was less."

"In what sense?"

"Less busyness. Less stress. Less putting my family second on my priority list. Less binge eating on unhealthy food because I didn't have the time to sit down and enjoy a real meal. My calendar was stacked, and I didn't have time for that. Or so I believed. Less relying on a glass or two of wine or whisky at the end of a long day to help me unwind and hopefully catch a few hours of sleep before I started all over again the next day. Less feeling like I had to work harder to reach this constantly unattainable goal of ... of what I'm not even sure."

"And the goal was to replace those things with more of the opposite?"

"Yes." Alex paused for a few seconds before continuing. He found this helped draw in the listener when he was about to say something important. "The goal became more quality time with my family. More time exercising and eating healthy. More time being present, in the moment, and enjoying each day. More time helping others."

This was his third podcast appearance this week, and he never got tired of talking about his journey, hoping it would inspire others who were feeling burnt out. He could empathize with people in that position. Alex felt like he finally had life figured out and wanted to pay it forward.

With the success of his last book, Alex created an online course that dug deeper into the concepts and tactics required to create a more customer-centric and innovative company. With a larger contingent of businesses reaching out to work with him, he was now more diligent and selective about which ones he would consult for.

For the companies that either could not afford his consulting services, or did not seem like a good fit, Alex would suggest they purchase his course and implement its strategies. It was a win-win. He never had to turn down any client. He had a viable option to serve whatever business came looking for his help. It was up to them to determine what option, if any, they wanted to take.

Creating, pricing, and promoting his online course, of course, was a whole new experience for Alex, as well. But he was enjoying each new challenge and the learning that came with it. The trick was to not go in blind and be forced to learn from personal mistakes.

For the course, he first performed a lot of market research. Were people interested in a course? If so, what made a good online course? Who was the target audience for the type of course he would be creating? What was the optimal price point that would make the course seem like there was value in the investment, but still not be cost prohibitive?

A lot of research and planning went into it before Alex determined there was an audience and a need for his course.

He also found out that the course did not need to be overly produced with videos shot at a studio and then edited by a professional. Sure, good quality video and audio would be required. His webcam was high resolution and produced a nice clear picture. His mic was not top of the line, but it gave him a clear sound that was pleasing to the ear. The course did not need to be professionally edited with amazing graphics and sound effects.

What people wanted were valuable tactics and tools they could easily apply themselves. So that is exactly what Alex game them in the course. Each tactic was explained clearly and concisely and the course provided resources like templates and cheat sheets they could utilize at any time for various situations.

But the biggest thing Alex learned when creating the course was to not let it take over his life. Creating the course never trumped one of his walks or date nights with Carolina. Creating the course never took priority over attending one of Martin's sporting events or father-son time fishing or hiking.

The goal was to produce another digital asset Alex could create once and sell a thousand times, so that he could have even more time with his family. Not less.

With his workshops, his consulting, his book, his online course, and his speaking engagements, Alex was on track to bring in $173k that year. For the first time, he would be projecting to make more money in a year than he did at DelTech.

But again, more money was not the goal. Alex often recalled the podcast he'd heard a few years back that talked about how once you reach a certain amount of income, no more amount of money could impact your happiness. What Alex was after was time. Quality time with Carolina and Martin. Everything he did was now intentionally designed around that goal.

On one podcast episode in particular where Alex was a guest, the host asked him to talk about some of the most influential people that supported or mentored him over the past few years.

Of course, Carolina was at the top of the list when it came to supporting him. If it was not for her, he would have given up early on. Perhaps he never would have even left DelTech.

There was Mikaela Brooks, the Marketing Manager at DelTech, who taught him about "niching" down and not presenting himself as a generalist.

He would never forget how Charles Redding took the time to meet with him and teach him how giving away free advice actually helps establish you as an expert and makes people want to work with you. Charles was also the first person to open Alex's eyes to the power of writing consistently on LinkedIn.

But it was Charles' approach to paying it forward that really stuck with Alex.

Another person that paid it forward and was instrumental in Alex's success was Sarah Emerson. She, too, took the time to meet with Alex and taught him the fundamentals about building a network on LinkedIn. This only helped reinforce the attitude of giving that Alex came to develop over time.

But on this particular podcast episode, Alex decided to give a special thanks to Pastor Johnson. It was Marcus that met with Alex on a few different occasions, not to mention the many Sunday sermons that had struck a chord with Alex.

"Which sermons in particular? Are there a few messages that stood out to you from certain Sunday mornings?" the host probed Alex for specifics. Both Alex and the host were Christians and enjoyed diving deeper into this topic.

"There are a definitely a few that stand out," Alex replied. "'Whoever loves money never has enough; whoever loves wealth is never satisfied with their income.'"

"From Ecclesiastes?"

"That's right. It opened my eyes about how I used to be all about money and material things. But so focused on 'things,' I was missing out on quality time with my family."

"That is powerful."

"Another one is from one of the Psalms. It was about teaching us to number our days so that we can have a heart of wisdom."

"Once we realize that time is ticking and we cannot get back each day that has gone by, it can sure change our outlook on how we spend our time."

"It sure did for me," Alex replied. "Again, I was spending my time seeking material things. I was not wise at all."

"Any more that stood out?"

"I could go on and on. But how about one more?"

"Go for it."

"This one from the apostle Paul is one of my favorites. He tells us to do nothing out of selfish ambition or vain conceit—"

"Rather, in humility value others above yourselves." Alex and the podcast host finished the statement in unison. It was one they both knew very well.

"That one has been huge for me," Alex explained. "Whether it is in my workshops, my consulting, my posts on LinkedIn, or whatever I am doing. I try to remember it's not all about me. It's all about helping others."

"That's a game changer."

"It sure is." Alex said this with a profound sense of learning. It was something that did not come naturally to him even a few short years ago.

When he started Align, Alex knew he would learn a lot about starting his business, marketing and selling his services, maintaining good cash flow, and so many other aspects of running a company that he never had to think about in his previous role at DelTech.

What Alex wasn't aware of was how much he would learn about himself. Only now did he come to understand that true fulfillment didn't come from prioritizing your life around money or the things money can buy. Alex now realized it was about making the most of the time and the gifts we have. It was about helping and serving others, even if we have to step out in a leap of faith.

When he thought back to who he used to be, Alex now saw he had a long way to go and so many areas where he needed to grow. He could not be more appreciative for everyone who had a hand in helping him get there.

But the journey was not over. In fact, it may only be just beginning.

You see, his LinkedIn following continued to grow, he was now up to over 18,000 followers and increasing every week. However, the types of questions that came Alex's way from his followers began to change.

More and more people were now interested in him and his journey. How did he do it? How had he managed to leave his corporate job and start his own one-man consulting business? How did he write a best-selling book and turn it into a course?

For every business leader that reached out to ask him about his work around customer-centricity and innovation, there were four people that connected to ask about his jump from the corporate world to solopreneurship.

So, naturally, Alex started to post about those things on LinkedIn.

At first, he would sprinkle in a post or two on some of these topics.

- ✔ The top 3 mistakes I made when starting my consulting practice.

- ✔ My number one tip for writing a best-selling book.

- ✔ The 5-step strategy I used to build my online course.

But what he soon found was that those posts were the ones that got the most engagement. By far. Not only that, but Alex felt much more comfortable sharing his journey, his strategies, and his tips for building a one-person business than he ever did sharing tactics around customer-centricity and innovation.

Was he qualified to be an authority on customer-centricity and innovation? He almost felt like an imposter when talking about those topics. Although he seemed to be on track to be a VP at DelTech, he never did reach an executive level position in a company. Did that mean he was not an expert? Should people take business-strategy advice from someone who never reached the pinnacle in that profession?

But with Align, Alex was the founder, the CEO, and the sole consultant. It was something he had built, with a lot of guidance and support from others, but he felt like he was much more of an expert in this area. Here he felt much more confident giving advice to others.

The icing on the cake for Alex was the most recent message he'd received from Rob Langley. "Hey Alex, it's been a while. I have been following your journey closely. As you know, I always respected your work here at DelTech. Your venture into starting your own consulting business has really got me thinking. Maybe that is something I should explore, as well. Do you have time for a chat so I can pick your brain a little?"

Maybe Alex's next venture would be to write a book about leaving the corporate world. Perhaps there was an online course in there somewhere about staring your own consulting business. Would there be demand for some workshops about writing and marketing a business book? Could he do some coaching for people that were looking to do what he did?

Perhaps Rob Langley would be his first client.

CHAPTER REFLECTION QUESTIONS

- ✔ Are you open to learning and growing, even if it means getting outside your comfort zone?
- ✔ What lessons are you currently learning that you can share with others to help them on their journey?

THE
PLAYBOOK

The 6 Steps to Solopreneurship

Here is the six-step playbook Alex followed in order to eventually build his successful solopreneur consulting practice:

1. Be the expert—determine your niche

2. Build credibility—network and offer services in exchange for learning and testimonials

3. Refine your offer—package and price your services like a product

4. Learn to sell—without customers/clients you have no business

5. Build an audience—via social media, podcast, newsletter, etc.

6. Build extra income streams (passive if possible)—through books, resources, courses, surveys, etc.

Solopreneur Lessons

Use these lessons Alex learned throughout his journey to help guide you through each step of your own path towards solopreneurship.

1. SOLOPRENEUR LESSON—NAYSAYERS

As a solopreneur, you will come across many naysayers.

- ✔ Learn to block them out.
- ✔ What someone else thinks of you is none of your business.

2. SOLOPRENEUR LESSON—YOUR NICHE

When starting any new business, be clear on the following:

- ✔ Who is my ideal client? (Be as specific as possible.)
- ✔ What is the specific challenge I help them solve?
- ✔ How will they benefit from my product/service?

✔ Why would they choose me, my product, or my service rather than the competition?

3. SOLOPRENEUR LESSON—TESTIMONIALS

Customer testimonials act as great social proof, building trust for new potential clients.

✔ Make sure your testimonials describe the challenges the customer was facing, the benefits they received, and why they chose you.

✔ Collect testimonials in the beginning by doing work for free or at a heavily discounted rate.

4. SOLOPRENEUR LESSON—CUSTOMER RESEARCH

All businesses can benefit from collecting feedback and insights from their customers.

✔ Get in the habit of doing this on a regular basis.

✔ Markets change. People change. Needs change.

✔ Never assume you know your customers' challenges and why they decide to buy a product or service.

5. SOLOPRENEUR LESSON—IMPOSTER SYNDROME

Every solopreneur is going to feel "imposter syndrome" at some point.

✔ Learn which challenges will be good for you to take on and grow your skillsets and which ones are truly over your head and could damage your reputation if you do a poor job.

6. SOLOPRENEUR LESSON—THE VALUE OF ROUTINE

✔ Having routine and structure is a good way to create healthy habits.

✔ Find ways to carve out focused time for important tasks each day.

7. SOLOPRENEUR LESSON—EMBRACE THE JOURNEY

Starting a business can be very stressful.

✔ Find ways to enjoy each day.

✔ Set small goals to achieve and celebrate regularly.

✔ Reward yourself with pockets of time doing things you enjoy.

8. SOLOPRENEUR LESSON—MENTORS

Pride is the burden of a foolish person.

✔ Being a solopreneur does not mean you have to figure everything out on your own.

✔ Seek out mentors who are a few years ahead of where you are in your journey.

9. SOLOPRENEUR LESSON—MORE CUSTOMER RESEARCH

Without customers, you have no business.

✔ In order to determine if there is a market for your product or service, test to see if people are willing to pay for it.

✔ If they are willing to pay for it, then continue to be curious.

✔ Learn as much as you can about them, their situation, their challenges, and what made them decide to pay for your product or service.

10. SOLOPRENEUR LESSON—GIVERS

There are plenty of giving people out there.

✔ Don't be afraid to reach out to others for advice.

✔ Some people may surprise you and be very giving with their time.

✔ Then, pay it forward and do the same for others.

11. SOLOPRENEUR LESSON—VIRTUAL ASSISTANTS

✔ Once you have established some processes, look to offload repeatable tasks, ones that are not a good fit for your strengths, or those that are not adding as much value for your time.

12. SOLOPRENEUR LESSON—BOOK STRATEGY

The three things you want to do really well with any book are the:

- ✔ Editing
- ✔ Design
- ✔ Promotion

Take the lessons Alex learned here and put a strategy in place when writing a book to help it look, read, and sell better.

13. SOLOPRENEUR LESSON—SCALING OPTIONS

At some point, you may be in a position to scale your business.

- ✔ Do you want to create a bigger company with employees?
- ✔ Or do you want to continue to invest in growing your personal brand?

Start by thinking about the lifestyle you want for yourself and go from there.

14. SOLOPRENEUR LESSON—LEVERAGING YOUR BOOK

- ✔ A book can be leveraged to create more assets that go along with it.
- ✔ Do some market research and determine other ways that you can leverage and monetize your book.

The Chapter Reflection Questions

In order to move away from a life of busyness and towards "the beauty of enough," use these questions found at the end of each chapter.

Chapter 1

- ✔ Have you ever found yourself in a situation similar to Alex's?

- ✔ Would you consider yourself a workaholic?

- ✔ How does it impact relationships with family and friends if you consistently prioritize work ahead of them?

- ✔ What are you doing to ensure your health is not neglected due to your work?

Chapter 2

- ✔ Does the idea of taking a vacation from work cause you stress, thinking about how much work will pile up while you are away?

- ✔ Do you have time in your calendar each day, each week, to allow yourself to think, to relax your brain?

- ✔ Have you ever gotten to the point where you know you need to make drastic changes in your work life in order to improve your home life?

Chapter 3

- ✔ Are you following a certain script for your life based on the expectations of others?

- ✔ Before deciding to start your own solopreneur journey, ask yourself what potential mentors you have in your network you can learn from.

- ✔ What specific gifts to you have to help solve a specific challenge for a specific group of people?

Chapter 4

- ✔ What networking groups can you join to expand your network and practice your pitch?

- ✔ What opportunities do you have to perform customer research?

- ✔ What type of service do you prefer to provide? Short or long engagements?

Workshops? Advisory consulting or hands-on implementation?

✔ What do you want your life to look like? How might you design your business around that?

Chapter 5

✔ What can you do to ensure you are finding joy in each day and embracing the journey?

✔ Do you have close family or friends that can provide support and motivation during the difficult times?

✔ How can you ensure you are in tune with your current or potential customers' needs, wants, and behaviors?

Chapter 6

✔ Are you leveraging social media to help create and identity and awareness of your brand?

✔ What tasks are you performing can be easily documented and delegated to someone else like a virtual assistant?

✔ What opportunities do you have to create assets you can sell so that you are not relying solely on selling your time for money?

Chapter 7

✔ Have you thought about how you might scale your business? What would that look like for you?

✔ What can you do to ensure you are not tempted to have your business take over your life? What boundaries can you put in place to prevent this?

Chapter 8

✔ Are you open to learning and growing? Even if it means getting outside your comfort zone?

✔ What lessons are you currently learning that you can share with others to help them on their journey?

Scripture References

There are several Scripture references throughout the book that play a part in Alex's journey. Each verse is listed below, in the order they appear in the book.

"Whoever loves money never has enough; whoever loves wealth is never satisfied with their income."

— *Ecclesiastes 5:10*

"For the love of money is a root of all kinds of evil."

— *1 Timothy 6:10*

"No one can serve two masters. Either you will hate the one and love the other, or you will be devoted to the one and despise the other. You cannot serve both God and money."

— *Matthew 6:24*

"Do not conform to the pattern of this world, but be transformed by the renewing of your mind."

— *Romans 12:2*

"We have different gifts, according to the grace given to each of us."

— Romans 12:6

"Blessed is the one who perseveres under trial because, having stood the test, that person will receive the crown of life that the Lord has promised to those who love him."

— James 1:12

"I have fought the good fight, I have finished the race, I have kept the faith."

– 2 Timothy 4:7

"The thief comes only to steal, kill, and destroy."

— John 10:10

"Do nothing out of selfish ambition or vain conceit. Rather, in humility value others above yourselves."

— Philippians 2:3

Acknowledgements

I would like to take this opportunity to give thanks to the great many people that helped, guided, supported, or inspired this book in various ways.

My wife, Cindy, for her continued support and encouragement to take on this endeavor and see it through. Cindy has been instrumental in giving me the boldness and perseverance to build Zero In, write my books, and use the gifts that God has given me.

Special thanks and praise must be given to Avner Landes. Avner has been much more than a terrific editor, but a guide, a coach, and a partner in this process. And to Sue A. Fairchild, who performed the proofread on the manuscript, correcting my spelling, grammar, formatting, and other mistakes to make the book that much more polished for you, the reader.

To the team at Miblart for the creative work on the book's graphics and design.

For the many BETA readers that agreed to read the original manuscript and provide insightful feedback. Because of you, the story, characters, and content of the book are all richer.

And, finally, to the many people who have inspired me over the past several years to continually grow, learn, and challenge my thinking. I have been blessed to connect, partner with, and get to know so many terrific people, many of whom inspired various aspects of this book.

About the Author

Dennis Geelen is the Founder of Zero In, a customer experience and innovation consulting company based in Peterborough, Ontario, Canada.

Through Zero In, Geelen works with companies and organizations that want to build engaging and loyal relationships with their customers as well as a culture of innovation with their employees.

Since founding Zero In during 2018, Geelen has worked with clients in industries ranging from government, non-profit, healthcare, insurance, technology, and energy, to sports and recreation.

Visit the Zero In website at
www.zero-in.ca.

Geelen also helps solopreneurs who are looking to build their own consulting or coaching practice.

To see how you can work with Dennis, visit
www.dennisgeelen.me

Made in the USA
Las Vegas, NV
24 September 2022